OUR GLOBAL LINGUA FRANCA
/ˈaʊɹ ˈɡloʊbəl ˈlɪŋɡwə ˈfɹæŋkə/

Also by Gregory V. Diehl

Everyone Is an Entrepreneur
Selling Economic Self-Determination in a Post-Soviet World

The Heroic and Exceptional Minority
A Guide to Mythological Self-Awareness and Growth

The Influential Author
*How and Why to Write, Publish, and Sell Nonfiction Books
that Matter*

Travel as Transformation
*Conquer the Limits of Culture to Discover Your Own
Identity*

Brand Identity Breakthrough
*How to Craft Your Company's Unique Story to Make Your
Products Irresistible*

OUR GLOBAL LINGUA FRANCA

An Educator's Guide to Spreading English Where EFL Doesn't Work

By
Gregory V. Diehl

For permission requests, write to the publisher at contact@identity-publications.com.

Connect with the author at www.gregorydiehl.net

Library of Congress Control Number: 2023914527

Orders by U.S. trade bookstores and wholesalers. Please contact Identity Publications: Tel: (805) 259-3724 or visit www.IdentityPublications.com

ISBN-13: 978-1-945884-77-1 (paperback)
ISBN-13: 978-1-945884-78-8 (hardcover)
ISBN-13: 978-1-945884-79-5 (ebook)

First Edition, published in Buffalo, Wyoming, by Identity Publications.

Cover art: The Tower of Babel, Flemish School, 17th Century, Sotheby's Lot.14. Public Domain.

For Hasmik, who made me care about the world of teaching (and the world itself) again.

———

"A long habit of not thinking a thing wrong gives it a superficial appearance of being right."

—THOMAS PAINE

———

TABLE OF CONTENTS

PREFACE

IN A RECENT small group English class, I asked my students, who ranged in age from late teens to early fifties, to describe the state of their country's public English education. After a brief discussion, they unanimously agreed that despite years of mandatory English classes, relatively few people reached adulthood being comfortable speaking or understanding any practical level of English. Those who *do* acquire at least conversational fluency will usually credit their competence to extra-curricular influences. My students saw their schooling as, at best, a heavily drawn-out way to get primed with the fundamentals of the English language. At worst, it wasted years of their lives, taught them explicitly wrong things about English, and made them resent having to learn the language at all.

Sadly, I've heard similar sentiments and seen the same consequences in every country I've taught in. These and countless other learners recognized that their teachers didn't speak enough English in class, so no real immersion occurred. When the teachers did speak English, they often did so with overt mistakes in pronunciation, vocabulary, and grammar. Consistent English use by a capable speaker should have been the classroom norm, with diversions into their native language only occurring to the extent necessary to facilitate understanding.

The same learners lamented that their teachers only taught from stale state-mandated books in an assigned fashion. They didn't use diverse activities to get anyone interested in learning in ways that would stimulate them differently or tailor their teaching to individual student needs. They knew they had to take control of their own learning and stop waiting for teachers to tell them how to get better at English, finding personally engaging English activities on their own.

Their schools, likewise, didn't offer enough opportunities for the learners to speak and express themselves in English. The English they put into practice was always a simplified and repetitive version of the language that relied on the same basic words and constructions that did not reflect real-world use. They realized they needed to put themselves in situations requiring them to use English in ways the phony conditions of the classroom did not prepare them for.

Finally, my students recognized their schools offered little motivation to *want* to learn English. Those in charge of their education primarily employed the threat of punishment for not receiving passing scores to graduate to the next level of schooling. Instead, the learners should have been encouraged with strong personal motivators to learn English well. Their teachers should have opened their eyes to how English would benefit them and made the learning rewarding at every stage.

One thing was clear: The system of EFL education they withstood was fundamentally flawed. Any approach to teaching English that consistently fails to produce English speakers is, in simple terms, not working. If we wish to improve our success rate and receive all the personal and social benefits that will arise from it, we must be willing to reconsider the standards and motivations for teaching English everywhere around the world.

INTRODUCTION
The Doorway to Global Communication

WHAT IS THE most important skill people worldwide can acquire to improve their material quality of life? What knowledge could we disperse virtually everywhere that would positively impact global society, regardless of cultural or economic circumstances? The answer most often overlooked is the vital skill of communication. For members of non-English-speaking countries, learning English offers the greatest potential for improving their communication and bears the fewest costs.

Like other universally useful areas of study (e.g., basic math and physics), people in virtually every position in life can benefit from learning to communicate better. It is a critical component of a universal education and a competent worldview. Those who learn to communicate with the rest of the world can be substantially happier, wealthier, and more connected than those who don't—all for a relatively small investment of time and effort.

The Modern Uniting of Tongues

In our modern age, communication is still commonly neglected across the globe. Relatively few people who stand to reap its benefits are actively doing so. How many problems could be fixed by little more than improving how we communicate? All knowledge and ability are affected and enabled by the power to communicate with others. Through mutual communication, we benefit from others' knowledge and ability while offering them the benefits of our own.

We can hardly apply what we know and can do if we cannot collaborate with others. Good communication skills form the catalyst that actualizes the social value of all other skills. Limiting your communication to only a relatively small population delineated by arbitrary borders diminishes your options to acquire what you want. How differently would a world where everyone could communicate effectively with each other look and operate? How might presently unsolved problems quickly be improved or resolved?

The Confusion of Tongues (otherwise known as the Babylonian Confusion of Languages or the Tower of Babel story) is a shared narrative template that has persisted across religious and historical texts, including the Bible[1] and ancient Greek[2] and Mesopotamian[3] myths. It tells of a time when everyone spoke a single language and, thus, could understand one another and work together and achieve common goals. Due to their pride and ambition, the gods became angry, "confounded the one language of the Earth into many, and scattered them

---

[1]   Genesis 11:5-8 KJV "And the Lord came down to see the city and the tower, which the children of men builded. And the Lord said, Behold, the people is one, and they have all one language; and this they begin to do: and now nothing will be restrained from them, which they have imagined to do. Go to, let us go down, and there confound their language, that they may not understand one another's speech. So the Lord scattered them abroad from thence upon the face of all the earth: and they left off to build the city."

[2]   In the myth of the Titans, one of the punishments enacted by the Olympian gods for the Titans' rebellion was forcing them to speak different languages so that they no longer understood each other. As well, in the story of Prometheus, who stole fire from the gods and gave it to humans, Zeus punished mankind by creating different languages so that they would not be able to work together against the gods.

[3]   Enmerkar and the Lord of Aratta is a Sumerian epic poem from the 21st century BC that includes an account of building a tower to the heavens and confusing the tongues of the people.

abroad." The once-unified people could no longer cooperate for the common good and had the progress of their civilization stifled by the forces in power over them. This myth illustrates how it becomes impossible for groups to collaborate on complex tasks once they can no longer communicate due to distance or differences in language and culture. We have been paying the price of unnecessary struggle and inefficiency brought about by poor communication.

The Growing Need for Global English

Because English is the most widely used and accessible language globally, its continuing spread as the global lingua franca[4] is our best option for dismantling arbitrary barriers to communication and the problems that stem from them. If we seek a future where all people can work to achieve common goals with equal opportunities, we should recognize that improving English education is among the most viable means to attain it. Our humanitarian duty is to consider improving EFL a top priority among other efforts to reduce suffering and raise living standards by empowering people to do more than they could before.

If people claim that they or their children don't have any use for English, it is another way of saying that they have learned to live in such a way that English is, apparently, not useful. They don't see how adding the ability to speak the world's most popular second language would aid them.

---

[4]   "Lingua franca" is an Italian term that translates to "Frankish language." English has a history of borrowing words from other languages because it has influences from many old language groups, such as Latin, Old Norse, French, and German. This contributes to its expressiveness and versatility.

The same can be true of anything, however. If you never learn how to cook, you will structure your life so you never have to cook. If no one around you can show you how to drive a car, you will learn to get around without driving, just like people did for millions of years before cars were invented. People who are blind or confined to wheelchairs can still navigate the world despite these objective limitations. People anywhere may have already learned to live well without the ability to communicate with the rest of the world, but that doesn't mean they would not still benefit from having the option and the opportunities it would bring.

The ability to communicate in English removes the most limitations from life with the smallest investment of time and effort compared to any other general skill. The ability to speak, write, and understand language is one of those generalized abilities that virtually everyone can benefit from. Still, an effective English teacher must understand that most people will only learn English if they see a pressing need for it.[5] A major part of an effective EFL teacher's job is to stoke interest and make their students aware of the benefits of learning. But the way English is conventionally taught virtually guarantees that only an exceptional minority of self-directed learners will ever achieve working fluency.

Governments throughout history have sought to promote literacy as a means of controlling and regulating populations through propaganda and indoctrination. I hope to demonstrate by the end of this book that just because something

---

[5] Linguistic constructivism proposes that learners actively construct their understanding of the world through experiences and interactions with their environment. Learning is most effective when learners can see the relevance and practical application of what they are learning and when they can apply their knowledge and skills to real-world, practical situations.

is a good idea, the way to implement it does not have to be through force and authoritarian oversight. I will argue that the path to sustainable progress in English education lies with self-aware educators finding better ways to present the benefits of learning and adopting better techniques for teaching. In time, more people will choose to learn English and other major world languages because they see it as a good way to achieve their wants and values.

A Note on Cultural Sensitivities

Nothing I have to say here directly relates to the cultural value of being able to speak a local native language. The ubiquity of English is undeniably linked to the checkered history of imperialism, as it was first introduced to many parts of the world through British colonialism, often being imposed on local populations, with both positive and negative consequences.[6] But we must maintain the mentality that its present ability to fill the planet's need for a universal bridge language extends beyond that incidental past for the good of everyone. And we must realize that there are better ways to spread new ways of thinking, acting, and communicating than through authoritarian force.

Rather than seeing this as a book about why everyone should favor global English over local languages, consider it a book about improving how the human race communicates and cooperates. Adopting modern globalized methods of thinking and acting does not contradict maintaining more traditional skills and approaches if that's what one chooses for themselves.[7] The will and autonomy of the individual

---

6   Phillipson, R. (1992). Linguistic imperialism. Oxford University Press.

7   Unless those traditions forbid operating outside them, in which case,

must be held in the highest regard when evaluating the ethics of cross-cultural linguistic influence.

It's not my goal to promote negative stereotypes of any given country or culture. Accordingly, I will sometimes refer to specific incidents and common practices in generalized ways. I will try to only specify the places, people, or languages involved when I consider it relevant to deriving the meaning from the experience or data I am referencing. Exactly where and among whom these things take place is mostly irrelevant to my points. What matters is that they are commonplace enough to be worth addressing.

I spent the first 18 years of my life in America. I was raised in American culture and still eagerly consume a good deal of it now. I speak American English and favor it above other variants.[8] This makes me unavoidably biased in teaching and evaluating the English language and foreign learners' competence in it. I trust the reader to discern how the advice I give and the lessons from my experiences best apply to their own situation—not that they will take my word as gospel and attempt to become my clone and mindlessly copy my approach to improving English education.

---

they are, in my humble opinion, coercive and should be disregarded for the good of the future generations whose personal development would be unfairly limited because of them.

[8] As well, it's been my experience that American English spelling, grammar, pronunciation, and terminology tend to be the most in-demand to learn and are seen as somewhat of an international standard for English in most countries (outside of Europe, where British English is largely preferred). The economic and cultural influence of the United States makes American English the preferred choice for casual, business, and scholarly communication.

A Note on EFL Training and Credentials

This book is not intended to serve as comprehensive training on how to teach English as a foreign language. It is not meant to replace TESOL/TEFL or any common EFL language training programs or certifications. It is meant only to complement and supplement the individual teacher's approach to and experience of helping foreign learners attain practical, conversational English fluency in whatever ways they see fit.

A lack of conventional credentials should not stop skilled English teachers from practicing their craft and contributing to English fluency. Technical certifications and even university degrees do not necessarily confer relevant knowledge and ability for teaching English. Under the wrong circumstances, they can detract from it because they might delude the credentialed teacher into assuming flawless competence for following instructions provided to them. So long as they are doing what they have been officially trained to do, they might feel they can do no wrong. They abdicate responsibility and stop analyzing the validity of their instruction. It's a major part of why EFL is in its present predicament worldwide.

This book references "traditional" or "conventional" English education worldwide. This generalization simplifies the poor global state of how English is taught to non-native speakers without having to go into the details behind every EFL approach on the planet (a task that would be impossible in the span of this book, anyway). My experience has been that mainstream language institutions almost always hold the same vital shortcomings in common, despite the diversity of schooling institutions worldwide. If the problems I describe here do not apply where you practice EFL, feel free to ignore what I have to say about them and focus on what's most relevant to your situation.

No one can offer a one-size-fits-all approach to language instruction. I've taught English or trained EFL instructors in a dozen countries[9] worldwide for all levels. I've traveled to and lived in dozens more than that. I've been exposed to all kinds of official and non-official educational circumstances, from elite schools in wealthy countries to indigenous communities in jungled settings. I've taught young children, teenagers, adults, and those approaching their elder years in private sessions and groups of several dozen. I've been given strict educational doctrines to follow and allowed free rein. You, too, can employ these principles in novel ways as you explore your educational settings.

---

[9] Armenia, China, Costa Rica, Ecuador, Ghana, Georgia, Indonesia, Iraq, Italy, Mexico, the Philippines, Spain, and Thailand are the countries in which I've been directly involved with foreign English education thus far. And I've managed to do all this without even acquiring a university degree.

CHAPTER 1

WHY ENGLISH?

ALL LANGUAGES ARE useful. Some are much more useful than others in specific circumstances. Learning any of them should be encouraged whenever someone has a valid external reason or internal passion for doing so. But lacking other inputs for deciding which language is definitively "best" to learn, English occupies a special place above all the rest.

English is the most objectively useful language in the world. The most people speak it in the widest variety of settings (as opposed to a language like Mandarin Chinese, which, while having a higher number of native speakers, is more limited to use within China). Speaking and understanding English, therefore, offers more new opportunities in travel, commerce, employment, relationships, art, and culture that are not available to people who only speak other lesser-used languages.[10]

We can think of languages as currencies of information. Major currencies like the dollar and euro are the most useful in our world economy. Virtually anyone you wish to buy things from anywhere in the world will either directly accept

---

[10]   There are, of course, other contenders for world languages worth spreading. Among them are Arabic, French, Mandarin Chinese, Russian, and Spanish, all of which function as regional lingua francas in one or more areas. Many of the principal arguments presented in this book for improving how we teach English can be carried over to improving how we teach other world languages.

dollars or euros or accept a currency that dollars and euros can easily be converted into. This is a direct analog of being able to speak English with people all over the world. Even if the people you want to communicate with *don't* speak English, you are not often far from someone who does and can translate for you. In the same way, you can exchange your dollars and euros for other currencies everywhere except in the most remote and underdeveloped places. That's not the case with most of the world's minor currencies. They will only ever be accepted in commerce within their nation of origin. You might have to go to great trouble even to find someone willing to exchange them for other currencies unless you are in a major city with international financial institutions.

The international community might poke fun at Americans and Britons for only speaking English instead of being multilingual (as is the norm in many other countries). However, their multilingual proficiency might not be due to their schools being better or their people having a stronger inherent passion for language. Their countries are smaller and closer to nations that speak other languages. It's a necessity of their geography, economy, and politics. There isn't an organic reason for most American and British people to become conversationally fluent in other languages. For most, English already suits their needs.

English Enhances Social and Economic Opportunities

English offers a lifeline to the people of the world who need opportunities the most. If even one member of a community, social circle, or family is conversationally fluent in English, it affords everyone connected to them new social and economic opportunities. The ability to form bonds of friendship, love, and culture depends on how well we can communicate. How are we supposed to share our values, philosophies, concerns, and wants in life if we cannot articulate our thoughts and emotions to people who might feel the same way? What if you meet your soulmate and they speak a different language than you? Finding someone to love is hard enough already. Why should we limit our prospects to only those who live near us and speak the same language? We can only marry someone who speaks English if we also speak English, even if it's the second or third language for both of us. And suppose you happen to be living in a culture with relationship values incompatible with your own. You then have extra incentive to focus your search for a partner outside your home country.

The opportunities opened up by speaking a major world language are even more clear in the professional world. A world-class doctor who doesn't know English might be quite limited in how they can practice. Their medical knowledge and skill alone won't enable them to communicate with patients and other doctors. An English-speaking doctor can practice in other countries or offer their services to foreigners who come to their country seeking treatment. Indeed, they may even monopolize the English-speaking market in their field if no one else offers their services in English. Their options for studying new developments in their field also increase, such as the types of treatment and technology they can offer, meaning their business will be more profitable and their patients healthier.

Consider the potential for improvement to the state of the global economy. How much unemployment and underemployment result from simple misalignment between which skills are perceived to be in demand and which are perceived to be available in the global labor force? The inability to communicate prevents simple and mutually beneficial economic exchanges from occurring. With even a rudimentary ability to speak a shared language, job opportunities might be more quickly filled by the people most qualified to do them who would otherwise be overlooked.

Speaking English is vital to many freelancers, self-employed workers, and entrepreneurs in the modern age. English is widely used in professional settings internationally and online. It is even a requirement of many modern types of in-office employment because employers want their staff to be prepared to deal with customers worldwide. For instance, English has been the standardized international language of air travel since 2001. All pilots, flight crews, air traffic controllers, etc., must be proficient in the language to do their jobs. Virtually any professional skill will be valued higher and more competitively on the market when a larger market of buyers can communicate in the language necessary to use it. This is just a manifestation of the economic law of supply and demand. Many workers are limited to employment at whatever rates are available in their local economy. By perusing job and freelancing sites in English, skilled people have many more opportunities to exchange their abilities for competitive wages.

Similarly, English spearheads many new technologies that are developed *by* speakers of major world languages and designed *for* speakers of major world languages. Though they may eventually be localized for members of every country who speak every language, people who can understand and use them earlier than those who cannot have a powerful social and economic advantage. Think of a new type of software that increases the efficiency of or obsoletes an entire class of human workers. Suppose Company A in Canada can accomplish the same thing by purchasing and implementing one new program that Company B in Cambodia requires hundreds of workers to do. There is nothing Company B can do to compete unless they, too, gain access to such revolutionary technology, which is likely to be available in English long before Khmer.[11]

English is even a pathway to learning other world languages. Suppose you only speak a local, uncommon language. Your options for finding a teacher who can teach some other local, uncommon languages in your native language will likely be limited. The probability that a teacher will happen to speak the two uncommon languages you require is small. What's much more likely is that a teacher of an uncommon language will cater primarily to people who speak one of the major world languages, English being the most prominent among them. You gain indirect access to the world's most obscure languages by having access to English. What if you want to learn Thai, Basque, or Swahili and speak only Welsh, Mongolian, or Pirahã? English is, in a way, a universal translator of languages. Learning it opens the door to all the other languages you might want to learn.

---

[11] This generality is especially true for modern digital technology like software and peripherals because using them is likely to require comprehensive abilities in the language they are tailored for. It's easy enough to figure out how to use a new type of water pump or saw—not so with cutting-edge design software or a virtual reality headset.

English Publishes More Information

Hundreds of years ago, the ability to read made little difference to the average person. There was not enough written information available. An illiterate today is at a major disadvantage for not being able to directly access all the valuable written information available to the rest of us. The same arguments for the merit of general literacy can be extended to a greater degree to English literacy. The modern non-speaker of English is in a similar state of information disconnect. More material is originally published in English or translated from other languages than any other world language. This includes the most philosophically and scientifically influential books from throughout history. Any modern English speaker can read a book, watch a video, or listen to an audio recording and receive information that can change their life—information they would otherwise have had no direct access to.

People who speak even a conversational level of English have considerably more opportunities for entertainment and education than those who don't. What should you do if you desperately want to watch, read, or listen to something not localized for your country?[12] As an English speaker with internet access, I can look up virtually anything I want to know how to do in mere moments. I can learn how a car engine works or how to clean a toilet. I can buy a tool I've never used and start building things I've never built before. I can look up the history of another country or begin studying the anatomy

---

[12] Even those recreational and educational materials that have been converted to other world languages from their original English with foreign subtitles or dubbing often suffer a loss of quality and meaning from how they were originally conveyed. There is always something extra to be gained by consuming media in its original language, even if it is nothing more than the artistic voice of the creator.

of the human brain. Attempting anything of the same sort is significantly harder in a less-prevalent language because the same educational resources aren't as available, and so the growth of local mentalities might be unfairly and unnecessarily bridled.

Have you ever tried to use a non-English version of Wikipedia? The difference in the number of articles and the quality/amount of information per article is staggering. At this time, Wikipedia's English database hosts 6.5 million articles. Meanwhile, the Armenian version of the site has only 300 thousand. There are more than 20 times as many English articles as Armenian ones. Already, we can see that Armenian-exclusive speakers are operating at a significant information disadvantage when they access a database like Wikipedia.

And what about the length and quality of those relatively few Armenian articles compared to their English counterparts? If I choose a broad and common topic of study at random, such as art history, it's easy to compare the Wikipedia articles in each language. The Armenian-language article[13] on art history contains only three paragraphs of information—barely 300 words and a few pictures. This is the type of broad article that we should expect many people throughout the general population to be interested in learning about. It's not something extremely narrow, esoteric, and specific that only a few specialists would be reading about. And still, the Armenian-speaking population of planet Earth is limited to just three paragraphs of general information about it on Wikipedia, the most popular repository of free knowledge on the internet. Having internet access already gives you an

---

[13]   https://hy.wikipedia.org/wiki/Արվեստի_պատմություն

enormous information advantage over people who lack it. Still, we can see how it's rather limited if you don't speak a language that the internet primarily caters to.

Meanwhile, the introduction to the English-language version of the Wikipedia article on art history is already longer than the Armenian version in its entirety. The English version contains a detailed breakdown of different styles and methods of art, different periods, different artists and categories, and so forth. It's 6,000 words long and contains numerous links to other articles on Wikipedia or external sites that contain more information about any of the sub-topics it covers. The names of all the famous artists throughout history have links to their own articles where you can click and learn more detail about each of them. The first art historian was some Greek guy named Pliny the Elder. He has his own Wikipedia article[14] just as long as the art history article you started on. Should you detour from your art history study to learn more about him? If you're reading the Armenian version of the site, you don't even have the option to pursue this emergent interest.

A complex, collaborative effort like Wikipedia, which crowdsources its content from global contributors, benefits from many minds. The greater the number of people who can contribute, the greater the potential for the quantity and quality of information. As there are far fewer people who can speak Armenian than can speak English, the total possible inputs for the Armenian version of the site will always be lower.

---

[14] https://en.wikipedia.org/wiki/Pliny_the_Elder

English Influences Cognition

There are obvious, well-documented cognitive benefits to becoming multilingual. What's less often considered is how our personality and sense of self can evolve due to our ability to think and communicate in fundamentally new ways. Many foreign learners have reported to me that learning English helped them get to know themselves better and express how they truly thought and felt because it gave them greater options for personal expression than they had had in their native language.

Linguistic relativity describes how the language a person thinks and communicates in influences their perception of the world and their cognition.[15] Grammatical structures and ways of phrasing basic concepts like time and space can create notable differences in how speakers of different languages perceive and talk about these things.[16] A language that lacks a precise vocabulary for distinguishing between shades of color, for instance, might influence native speakers to pay less attention to these distinctions because they don't have convenient labels. The freedoms and limitations of your native language undoubtedly bias you in some ways and open your mind in others.

Think of how many interesting, beautiful, or useful words you might know in other languages that cannot be translat-

---

[15] Otherwise known as the Sapir-Whorf hypothesis, developed by Edward Sapir and Benjamin Lee Whorf in the 1930s. The consensus among linguists seems to be that at least a "weak" version of this idea is demonstrable across populations. My own observation across languages and cultures inclines me to believe that people are susceptible to cognitive conditioning based on exposure to the use of language, which goes on to affect culture, which in turn affects language in an eternal incestuous cycle.

[16] Casasanto, D., & Boroditsky, L. (2008). Time in the Mind: Using Space to Think about Time. Cognition, 106(2), 579-593.

ed into English except as drawn-out phrases. The Japanese term "wabi-sabi" (侘寂) could be described in English as recognizing the beauty of impermanence and imperfection in things. The German word "schadenfreude" means taking joy in another person's suffering. I can explain these concepts to you in English the way I just did. Still, it would certainly be more convenient to refer to them as single words denoting an intangible feeling or state of being that all English speakers would immediately relate to through personal experience. Once you have an established category and verbal referent for a concept, it is more cognitively convenient for you to think about it and use it as an ingredient in your original thoughts. That's one of the reasons that English has borrowed so many words and phrases from other languages and incorporated them into the common lexicon; it's frequently easier than inventing new terms from scratch and liberates us to begin using these distinctions at will in our discourse in ways that less-flexible languages cannot. As a result, English now has an infamously large vocabulary, which means more ways to conveniently refer to reality and concepts that might be totally absent in other languages.[17]

---

[17] I sometimes coin my own English terms when I find that I need to refer to something for which a convenient term does not already exist, such as "ideollergic reaction" (a portmanteau of "ideological allergic reaction," indicating when someone's ideological immune system erroneously treats harmless foreign ideas as harmful), "margin of idiot" (a specialized application of "margin of error" that describes to the likelihood that some intelligent human actor will do something idiotic that negatively affects the outcome of a plan), and "paragraphical mitosis" (when a long paragraph gets split into multiple smaller ones in the process of editing). I even came up with an idiom to describe a state of frustration I felt while comparing my ability to speak a new language to my proficiency in English. I felt "like Mozart trying to play the tuba," which describes when someone adept at something regresses to a novice level at something else related but for which there isn't an adequate transfer of skill.

English is an incredibly nuanced, varied, and flexible language, which makes it comparatively effective for building an advanced internal understanding of oneself and conveying it to others. English can radically improve cognitive self-awareness and emotional intelligence because it offers more options for reflecting on what one is thinking and feeling and how best to express these essential aspects of self. Attempting the same in their native tongue often left my students feeling that something was lacking or that it was too awkward to get things across in the same way. Even though English was their second language, they still found it was better suited for expressing some important truths they couldn't find equivalents for in their native tongue. If their native language lacks linguistic categories or distinctions that exist in English, the learner may initially struggle to perceive or differentiate certain concepts or objects. But in approaching English fluency, their mind will grow more open to thinking differently. The grammatical rules, vocabulary, and idiomatic expressions of English can enhance how they process and convey subjectively important meaning.

The English learners I've helped approach fluency have reported many benefits to their personality and mentality as a result of their linguistic proficiency. Many have said their confidence increases when speaking English but goes back down when using their native language. How they assess a situation and what actions they should take will change depending on what language they are thinking in or how they are articulating their thought process to someone else. Their "English mind" often perceives that there is more information to take in and more ways to think about possible strategies and appropriate behavior, to the point that their "native language mind" doesn't even seem to them like it is capable of assessing things fairly and considering all information. Some automatically switch to English when thinking or talking about science because so much more scientific discovery and vernacular have been established in English. Or they might use English to talk about private and sensitive things that there is no precedent for discussing natively. A new side of their personality emerges as a result.

Some have reported predominantly thinking first in English instead of their native language, even while still living in their home country and interacting with others who speak it. They developed this habit because they found it more cognitively liberating to have English's vocabulary, expressions, and flexible grammar as their primary tool for conceptualizing the world compared to the limitations they encountered when trying to do the same in their native tongue. They express their feelings and autognosis (i.e., self-knowledge) more comfortably and accurately in ways that lack native equivalents. These individuals called English "the language of their soul," while their native languages remained cherished frameworks through which to recall and express their childhoods and home-life associations.

There can even be an isolationist effect that a foreign English speaker associates with their native language once they become aware of external options for learning and communicating through English. Many describe their home country and the culture and language associated with it as "a separate planet" that operates with its own isolated rules and ideas, largely cut off from the rest of the world. English is the doorway that enables them to experience everything outside the narrow worldview of home and everything they are capable of creating within the confines of their own minds.

English Loosens Cultural Limitations

For months, I lived among a family in China and offered full-time private tutoring to their teenage children and experienced Chinese life and culture from an intimate point of view. Years of conventional EFL education in school had only imparted these bright children with basic English abilities. The caring parents recognized that their children would never become conversationally fluent without a new approach that would immerse them in practical English use every day. As this family was planning on immigrating to America soon, they needed their children to be good English speakers for visa approval. Their motivation to get out of the country was their concern over increasing cultural and legal restrictions. They knew they could not create the free life they wanted for their kids unless they could continue raising them in a more open-minded place. They saw learning English as the key to a future free of cultural and legal imposition for their children.

If you grow up thinking there's only one way that people can work, be in relationships, raise their children, shape their spiritual beliefs, and so on, you're biased toward living within those limitations. It's normal for you and perhaps what you see as the only viable option. But suppose you become aware that people in other parts of the world do things differently, that there are countless valid approaches to every aspect of modern life. You'll be much less likely to mindlessly accept how the people around you happen to think and act, which is a form of cultural enmeshment.[18] And there might

---

[18] "Enmeshment" is a psychological term that describes a lack of personal boundaries and undifferentiated sense of identity with others that causes loss of or delayed autonomous development, distinctiveness, and self-direction.

be ways to live that you would find much more meaningful and fulfilling than what your culture expects of you. Your mind will be irreversibly opened just by the awareness that other options exist.

Take cultural (and often contentious) conceptions of marriage. Lacking other cultural influences about how relationships can work, young women in some cultures are more likely to accept that it is okay for men to kidnap them, rape them, and force them to marry and bear numerous children at their husband's behest. This is an accepted or perhaps merely "frowned-upon" practice in many parts of the world. It is not treated as the objective violation of bodily autonomy and human rights it is. You can apply the same logic to the most inhumane practices still taking place in the world, such as culturally condoned forms of torture, slavery, and genital mutilation. What happens when you learn that people in some other cultures consider these "normal" practices to be cruel, insane, or criminal? Once you know it is possible not to live this way, you might realize that what's normal for everyone around you might be undesirable for who you are. It's not in line with your authentic self. You might begin to accept that you can make your own choices about the most important aspects of your life and seek something better. You can discover your own intrinsic personality and values. You can choose your own destiny, whether that's applied to personal lifestyle preferences, like letting your pet dog sleep in your bed because you saw someone in a foreign movie do it, or major philosophical fundamentals like basic respect for autonomy. Learning English can be a way for people to get out of systems of restricted or coerced relationships of any kind.[19]

---

[19] This is broadly true of all kinds of education, but particularly for learning

Operating exclusively in a local language that is largely isolated from the accumulated wisdom of history, art, and science practically guarantees a strictly localized sense of cultural identity, with all its limitations. The evidence of this is that culture rapidly changes in places with access to media and education from the rest of the world. As societies become more educated and affluent, they prioritize self-expression, autonomy, and personal fulfillment over traditional values like obedience, conformity, and social order.[20] The local populace starts thinking differently because it has new influences to contribute to its sense of what exists, what is possible, and what is desirable. It has a wider array of inputs to rearrange and pick from. The newer generations become aware that there is more than one way they can think about something… more than one way to build their lives and act instead of defaulting to the same values as the generation that preceded them. This enables and expedites the process of self-actualization for each individual.[21]

It's no secret that extra-cultural influence is one of the arguments often used *against* learning English and other major world languages. Authority figures frequently don't want young people to consume certain kinds of movies, television

---

to communicate in a major world language, for reasons that should already be clear. Consider the Malala Fund, an organization that advocates for girls' education around the world. It was founded in 2013 by Malala Yousafzai, a Pakistani activist who was shot by the Taliban for speaking out in favor of girls' education and freedom from the restrictive rules of her society.

[20] Inglehart, R. (1997). Modernization and postmodernization: Cultural, economic, and political change in 43 societies. Princeton University Press.

[21] According to Maslow's hierarchy of needs, self-actualization refers to the process by which someone reaches their highest potential and fulfills their highest values. These will be different for each individual. A prerequisite to this is discovering what someone's potential and values truly are.

shows, books, and music because they fear the effects of foreign influence, often for no other reason than that they are different from what the local culture has embraced as normal. The more enlightened among them may want young people to learn English for practical reasons, but they still don't want them to be influenced by any foreign values.

These people want to eat their cake and have it too. You cannot open your mind to global communication without accepting the possibility that some information you don't like will make it through the doorway. Only dictators have the power to staunch the flow of information to repressed populations, and even they still fail to make their firewalls totally effective against the spread of knowledge and cultural influence. Imposing linguistic limitations is a more subtle and politically correct form of modern book burning: The goal is to restrict the development of personality and identity by restricting independent thought.[22] By learning English, you're virtually guaranteed to be exposed to some elements of foreign cultural values.[23] No other language produces or promulgates media that is so widespread among foreign cultures and speakers of foreign languages. It will affect the way

---

[22] The most famous example of imposed linguistic limitations in fiction is probably Newspeak in George Orwell's dystopian novel *1984*. Newspeak is the official language of a totalitarian society, and its purpose is to limit freedom of thought and expression by enforcing cognitive dissonance, simplifying grammar, and eliminating concepts that could undermine the government's authority and ideology.

[23] A surface analysis might tempt the reader to conclude that I am promoting the spread of exclusively Western cultural values at the expense of various local ways of life in pursuit of global cultural homogeneity. *All* forms of cultural value become more accessible when the doorway to global communication is opened. Each individual is more free to decide for themselves which values and practices are most in line with their own authentic identity, regardless of their history or in which part of the world they originate. Gatekept and compartmentalized perspectives become available to everyone.

you think. It might cause you to question how the people around you think and do things by default, either by offering a superior alternative or criticizing the local norm. This is an exciting opportunity for personal growth and may even be one of the primary reasons a foreign learner is motivated to get better at English.[24]

Of course, you can learn to speak English and still end up agreeing with the values of your local culture. But you will then at least have the option to disagree. You can be exposed to other cultural ideals and consciously reject them. You will have greater choice than someone who cannot even introduce them to their consciousness due to linguistic barriers. The goal is not the suppression of local cultural identities, but neither is it their protection of them at the expense of the individual's authentic self-expression.

---

[24] I often incorporate English-language media into my instruction for reasons that go beyond exposure to the language. Books and movies help learners think differently, discover more about themselves, and use English to articulate their uncovered values. One young woman I worked with had the profound realization that she didn't want to take on the kind of traditional marriage role expected in her culture after watching *A Walk to Remember* and *The Notebook*, the 2002 and 2004 films based on Nicholas Sparks' romantic novels of the same names. This gave her organic reasons to use new English terms related to intimacy because she was now expressing something of deep personal importance.

CHAPTER 2

BROKEN EFL CONVENTIONS

ISN'T ENGLISH ALREADY being taught as a foreign language throughout the world? Isn't this problem already being addressed? To a degree, yes. But what is called English education often has little to do with learning anything of substance or practical utility.

Conventional EFL instruction revolves around forced, unnatural, and artificially prompted English. The thinking seems to be that as long as students are being exposed to English in any form, they are learning it. Learning is often measured more by input (i.e., how much time and effort are spent on study) than by output (i.e., how much practical English knowledge and ability the students end up with). Many years of repetitive English training might amount to little more than memorizing lists of English vocabulary, popular phrases, and grammatical rules by rote, which is often all that English exams are designed to measure. They are meant more to get students accepted to universities through good grades and high standardized test scores than to help them become capable English speakers. Accordingly, EFL teachers merely pile English content into students' heads and drill them until they can replicate it on command.

At a private school in the Kurdish region of Iraq, I noticed the strong academic focus on preparing the children of wealthy parents for enrollment at universities in international locations across Western Europe. Their metrics for success were based only on the test scores that international universities would consider in their admissions processes. Accordingly, parents and the school administration were desperate to make them look impressive to overseas educational bodies. Actually learning to use English to form and communicate original thoughts was a secondary concern.

At times, I have found alternative schools that explicitly sought an unconventional approach, such as one Montessori-style[25] elementary school in northern Italy. In hindsight, it became clear to me that there was something these schools liked only about the *image* of a progressive approach to English education. They were attracted to these ideals as concepts because they recognized, on some level, that the conventional approach was inadequate. But they didn't have any means to implement systemic changes. It was too big a break from tradition, bureaucracy, and cultural norms.

One might expect the local populace to embrace new approaches in places where education opportunities are rare, such as rural villages in developing countries. Instead, I have often witnessed schools that feel threatened by the intrusion of native English speakers that make the local approach seem inadequate. Their meager institutions are more concerned with preserving their reputation than serving the children's educational interests. I've faced uphill battles spreading positive English-language influence in such places, even when they paid lip service to improvement. The fact that these places bother to have English teachers and mandate years of

---

[25]   Dr. Maria Montessori was an Italian physician and educator who promoted a child-centered learning environment based on self-directed learning and hands-on exploration.

English study for their children should be a sign that they at least understand the value of learning English. So why wouldn't they want to take advantage of every opportunity to accomplish that goal faster and more comprehensively? It only begins to make sense when you accept that learning English is not their goal. They have no imperative to improve.

I've learned from these experiences that change primarily comes from outside the established schooling systems. It often happens best via independent teachers who are free to improve how things are done. Teachers and students often aren't aware of shortcomings with the conventional methodology. They don't know that there are better alternatives — so they never seek them. No one will ever be motivated to fix a systemic problem they've grown accustomed to, and superior educational options cannot enter societies that oppose improvement.

The Broken Template

It often goes understated how much of what is taught about the grammar, vocabulary, spelling, punctuation, and pronunciation of English is objectively incorrect. Furthermore, much of what is taught that is technically correct (in that it forms a grammatically valid English sentence) is still awkward, impractical, inefficient, or counterproductive.

Non-native teachers often speak only broken English. They teach predominantly in their native language because they don't know enough English. This habit robs students of two vital language learning components: (1) At least one reliable example of how the English language sounds and works, and (2) the opportunity to be naturally engaged in the language. It's like making an imperfect copy of an imperfect copy of a series of imperfect copies. If each new generation of English speakers is only influenced by the imperfect generation of English speakers that came before them, the mistakes compound and mutate over time. Similar and progressively worse pronunciation, spelling, grammar, and vocabulary errors replicate throughout the culture; no one employs a standard of clear and articulate native English to compare them to.

That's why it can seem like each part of the world has its unique collection of English errors that almost everyone there makes. These errors stand out to native ears, but the people making them are unaware that they are doing anything wrong. You can somewhat accurately identify where a person is from (and where they learned their English) based on how they use the language incorrectly. A part of this, of course, is a usually strong foreign accent, but it also shows up more subtly in small errors in grammar and inappropriate use of common words. Different styles of poor English become like a linguistic fingerprint of where a foreign English speaker originated.

How many of these common English errors do you recognize from foreign learners?

- Misusing common expressions (e.g., "Thanks, God." instead of "**Thank** God.")[26]

---

[26] "Thank God" is an interjection that can be thought of as conjugated in either the imperative or subjunctive mood. Imperative indicates that you are giving a command for someone to thank God. Subjunctive expresses it as a wish or hypothetical with some of the archaic phrasing merely implied, e.g., "(May we) thank God." or "(Would that we) thank God." However, the incorrect phrasing of "Thanks, God." indicates that you are directly addressing God and thanking Him in a bemusingly casual way.

- Misplacing possessive nouns and prepositions (e.g., "That's a Michael's picture." instead of "That's a picture **of** Michael.")[27]
- Not knowing when a verb would be better with a direct object (e.g., "Buy me." instead of "Buy me **this**.")[28]
- Not knowing when a verb needs a preposition to indicate its indirect object (e.g., "Explain me how it works." instead of "Explain **to** me how it works.")[29]
- Omitting the auxiliary verb "do" (e.g., "How I missed that?" instead of "How **did** I miss that?" or "I not missed that." instead of "I **did** not miss that.")[30]
- Conjugating both of two verbs working together instead of just the first (e.g., "How **did** I **missed** that?" for the auxiliary "do" example or "I **decided** to **walked**." instead of "I decided to **walk**.")[31]

---

[27] "Michael's picture" is possessive and indicates the picture belongs to Michael. "Picture of Michael" indicates what the picture depicts: Michael.

[28] Saying "buy me" without a direct object means that *you* are the direct object instead of the indirect object, the thing receiving the action by being bought. "Buy me this." makes "this" the thing being bought. There is an implied preposition when the indirect object comes first, indicating that you are the one whom "this" is being bought **for**. If you are going to omit the direct object, it would be better to include the preposition to remove any ambiguity (e.g., "Buy **for** me."). Most confusingly, some verbs work both with and without direct objects, such as "to hide." You can say "Steve hides" as well as "Steve hides his money," but the meaning is totally different.

[29] If I am "explaining you," it means I am talking about you. If there is something I am "explaining **to** you," it means I am talking about something else (in this case, "how it works") while addressing you. Similarly, I can either "await you" or "wait **for** you," but I cannot "wait you."

[30] We use "do" as an auxiliary verb when asking present or past simple questions, negating statements, and sometimes when placing emphasis on positive statements (e.g., "Yes, you're right, indeed I **did** miss that.")

[31] We only conjugate the verb that comes first and leave the rest unconjugated. In this case, it should be "How did I **miss** that?"

One fun and depressing exercise you can do is open the English teaching material of almost any given country's mass-produced curriculum to a random page. See how many English errors you can spot at a glance. Can you even find a single page that does not contain grammar, spelling, or punctuation mistakes? It may be a missing comma on one page or entirely wrong ways to conjugate common English phrases on others.

The people who oversee the creation of textbooks and dictate the curriculum for educational institutions should have plenty of incentive to proofread and fix their work before publishing. How hard would it be to hire a competent native English proofreader to review their educational textbooks and other learning materials before they are printed and distributed? In the digital age, there is no excuse for such negligence, even if there are no native English speakers present on their staff. The internet makes it easy to outsource the task to qualified professionals worldwide.

The potential for societal harm from such careless oversight is enormous. These mass-produced educational materials will form the foundation for how an entire generation learns and uses English for the rest of their lives. Those who learn English incorrectly will be handicapped in their attempts to participate in a global society because they will not be able to communicate as well as they should. Yet, the authorities are unreceptive to correction. Once someone has accepted doing something the wrong way, they are unlikely to ever be open to improving it.

Inappropriate Metrics of Success

Conventional English exams monitor if students have memorized a certain grammatical concept or the vocabulary word for a given situation that the exam designers have contrived for easy analysis. That's one reason few people recognize a systemic problem: They are measuring the wrong things. On the surface, exams seem like a reasonable way to assess how well masses of students have learned something about English. But once the testing date has passed or the class has been completed, what was memorized is primed to be forgotten. The students' incentive is now to clear space to focus on what's required for the next class or exam.

The Common European Framework of Reference for Languages (CEFR) is a frequently used standard for assessing student proficiency in a foreign language. It consists of six levels of language proficiency, ranging from A1 to C2. A1 or A2 beginner English learners should be able to understand and use familiar everyday expressions and basic phrases. B1 or B2 intermediate English learners should be able to describe their thoughts, interests, and experiences related to common topics of conversation and elaborate at least briefly upon them. Finally, C1 or C2 advanced English learners should be able to express themselves spontaneously and produce and analyze detailed technical writing on a wide range of topics as they approach fluency.

While proficiency metrics like CEFR can be useful for schools, employers, and other organizations to get a general idea of someone's English ability, they are inappropriate as absolute standards by which to shape EFL. They offer only broad frameworks that are biased by the priorities of the authorities that design them. "My school says my English level is C1," is as reliable a metric as "my grandma says I'm handsome."

Such frameworks cannot account for each student's linguistic needs and interests. They are designed to advance English students to the next stage of schooling. They cannot account for an individual's motivation, personality, cultural background, experience, and communication aspirations. I've known many English learners labeled at intermediate or advanced levels who were still making basic conjugation and pronunciation errors in every conversation. They seemed quite uncomfortable using English with native speakers in an uncontrolled environment outside the classroom. What good is it for such students to perform well on homework and exams but flounder when talking to English speakers in the real world?

It is often even the case that the longer that students spend studying English, the worse they get at it. In any other domain of learning or practice, we would take this as an obvious sign there is something wrong with the methodology employed. If following the advice of your football coach for years only causes you to get worse at football, you need a new coach. If your doctor's prescriptions consistently make your health worse, your doctor should not be practicing medicine. But when it comes to EFL, the problem is generally ignored. If acknowledged, blame is placed on the students for "not trying hard enough" and failing to conform to their demands. It's never even considered that there could be something wrong with the instructions or how they are given. Right practice should lead to right results. In the domain of English education, right results are conversational fluency and practical communication.

But still, isn't any English education better than none at all? No, not necessarily. Learning the wrong things (or even the right things in the wrong ways) impedes learning. It might disincentivize students from learning correctly. It might entrain bad habits and inaccurate information, which will bias learners against acquiring good habits and accurate knowledge. It will also waste time, energy, and other resources that could have been spent on other valuable pursuits. Doing nothing is better than doing the wrong thing. Acting without a competent strategy can do more harm than good.

Students who have studied English for years in school might be fortunate enough to become familiar with the basics and generalities of English. They might understand common words and phrases or be able to recite a mundane conversation by rote. But that is generally all they have to show for their years of investment into a counterproductive system that thrives on keeping everyone busy.

Students who independently commit to English self-study or who expose themselves to English-language media have much better examples of how English works than those who rely on appointed authorities.[32] This can lead to conflict and confusion with the conventional EFL system. Who should learners trust more? A celebrity on TV? A strange tourist visiting their country? Or the people they spend eight hours a day with and whose orders they are trained to follow? It can be quite a hurdle for young learners to accept that they must look outside their schools for better English influence. Learners might even erroneously think of themselves as being bad at English because they don't conform to their teachers' broken standards.

---

[32] It's my conjecture that Hollywood movies and celebrities have inadvertently done more to increase global English ability (and international communication as a whole) than all the EFL teachers around the world combined.

Linguistic Hubris

The flawed standards of EFL education create a harmful dichotomy between two incompatible versions of English. Students can have high *assessed* competence in the fake school version of English. They can also have high *practical* competence in real English as it is used worldwide. To make progress in one is often to sacrifice it in the other.

I have given presentations in high schools and universities about the benefits of supplementing mandatory English classes with conversation-based English immersion. Predictably, the greatest interest always came from the students who liked English but didn't learn well via the school's approach. But another kind of unanticipated response also occurred several times across my presentations. Students who received high marks in school seemed offended by the idea of a better way to learn. They did not want to consider their hard work to be inadequate or counterproductive. Ironically, they were making basic English errors while verbally protesting the idea that their EFL was lacking and were not receptive to correction.

These students had already received social recognition for their supposedly good English ability, so correction challenged their sense of pride in this false competence. It's also revealing that these students, who trusted their teachers to lead them in learning English, wouldn't at least consider that a native speaker could have advice worth listening to about the language. Those who think they already know are far less likely to learn, even if given a better opportunity to. There will be too much cognitive dissonance[33] to overcome.

---

[33] Cognitive dissonance is a psychological term that describes the mental stress incurred from holding simultaneous contradictory ideas consciously in mind. It's one reason we are likely to ignore or reject information that contradicts what we already believe.

Effective English teachers focus their curriculum on what is essential for their students' developmental stage. But this is impossible for even the best teachers if they work within a fixed model that prevents deviation from the prescribed curriculum. Teachers need to be free to diagnose the level of understanding their students have and what approach will help them achieve the next stage of practical competence.

Methodology aside, many countries must improve their general cultural mentality about English before systemic progress can occur. As noted, many parents believe that it would be better for their children *not* to learn English. They don't want them to have the option of leaving their home country for greener pastures or being exposed to too much foreign cultural influence. They believe their children and country would be better off limiting their communication opportunities to local influences and denying themselves the benefits of international exchange.

It's enough to make one wonder if conventional English education might be intentionally designed to be ineffective. Even if the practical results are minimal, schools still get credit for attempting. After all, the governments of developing countries may have a proprietary interest in keeping citizens within their borders. Should those underprivileged individuals be made to sacrifice what would be best for themselves so that their political leaders can make those choices for them? Should they be forced into the same boat as their countrymen? Or should we encourage and enable them to pursue every opportunity they develop the ambition for?

CHAPTER 3

CONVERSATIONAL FLUENCY AS THE METRIC FOR SUCCESS

LEARNING A LANGUAGE isn't just memorizing the concepts, sounds, and symbols related to it. It is changing yourself to perceive, conceptualize, and interact with the world differently.[34] Language is our primary tool of thought, so learning a new language means learning to think differently. English learners need opportunities to practice using the language in meaningful ways in order to develop communicative competence. Achieving conversational English fluency means reaching a state of unconscious competence in this new way of thinking.

Fluency is unconscious and automatic cognition of the world in English. It involves the ability to process language quickly while engaging in other cognitive processes. Effortlessness is key. You don't just want to memorize a lot of words. You don't even necessarily want to be a great translator between English and your native language. What you want is to look at a chair and know that it is a "chair" in English just the same as you might know that it is a "kursiun" (كرسي) in Arabic, "chaise" in French, "yǐzi" (椅子) in Manda-

---

[34] A better way to describe the process would be "adopting," "acquiring," or "acclimating to" a language.

rin, "stul" (стул) in Russian, or "silla" in Spanish. You want to be able to perceive and think about the world in English.

The fluency-seeking learner should pursue the ability to say what they think with fluidity instead of slogging through the delay of internal translation between English and their native language. They can best do that by being immersed in the language, hearing it, and interacting with people actively speaking it. Eventually, they start to think, "Oh, yes, this is a spoon. I've heard that English word being used enough times in contexts where people were clearly referring to the little round utensil I eat soup and ice cream with, my trusty little miniature shovel. I understand now that my friend on the other side of the dining table wants me to hand him a spoon when he uses that word in this context."

The conversationally fluent English speaker mostly no longer has to think about what they are saying or hearing. They mostly no longer need to translate between English and their native language because it has become an unconscious process (at least until they encounter some uncommon words or constructions that they haven't already adapted to). Their social settings instill in them what will be most useful for them to learn next.[35] Learners must be in positions to use English to attempt to get something they want from the world. The task of the foreign language teacher is to oversee this process, introducing new words and increasingly complex structures as needed while guiding learners under controlled social conditions. The eventual outcome is conversational English fluency.

---

[35] The social interactionist theory of language acquisition proposes that language is primarily learned as a social phenomenon as the result of interaction with others.

The Purported Difficulty of Learning English

There is a false premise upon which a great amount of conventional foreign English education is built: the idea that it is difficult to learn English compared to other world languages. And because the learning process is supposedly so difficult, it must be bureaucratized, micromanaged, and forced upon learners to be effective at all. English is not inherently more complex or difficult in most aspects compared to other common world languages. We simply lack guides who know how to consciously teach it well. Countless people learn English in natural contexts across the globe every day. They also learn other languages that are objectively *more* complex with a similar level of ease—all without ever setting foot in a language classroom.

Of course, that's not to suggest that there aren't some particular quirks about English that set it apart. English speakers are notorious for their wild spelling. We borrow many words and conventions from other languages, so we don't get to be content with just one set of phonetic patterns. Our common vocabulary is vast, which is to say nothing of our uncommon vocabulary. We even have this nasty habit of combining different parts of speech to create emergent grammar, such as the case with phrasal verbs like "to break up" or "to get around to."

But what's often overlooked is that English is also a lot easier in some ways than other languages. We don't add gender to nouns, adjectives, and articles, for instance. We rely more on the order of words than anything else to make relationships clear, which makes conjugating complex sentences vastly simpler. We mostly add "will" before the equivalent present tense for conjugating future tenses. English also doesn't require a precise tonal system in its pronunciation to get semantic meaning across in words, which would make even learning the alphabet itself much more complicated.

That English is difficult to learn is a particularly harmful superstition. Perpetuating it can bias English learners against the language. It can turn them off from trying as earnestly as they would. It can make the learning process seem harder than it is, even as learners are actively engaged in it and facing the same difficulties they would with most any other language. It's a self-fulfilling prophecy; the belief that English is difficult to learn prompts us to adopt approaches that make it as difficult as we presume it is.

If English were inherently difficult to learn, we would only ever see it happening under conditions of expert instruction and constantly enforced studying. Instead, the opposite is true: More people worldwide are learning English every day than any other language. It does typically get harder to learn English as one gets older. It's easier for children to pick up new languages because they're more adaptable and curious than adults and the elderly. They have greater sensitivity to the use of language around them. But it is still possible to show older folks that their lives will be better with enhanced linguistic abilities. And indeed, older people have some distinct English-learning advantages over children, such as generally better studying habits and greater capacity for cognitive reasoning.

The Limits of English by Rote

The word "rote" indicates the use of memory, usually with little intelligence. It is learning via unthinking routine or repetition, i.e., simple conditioning. But minds are not computers. You cannot upload data files and install programs at will.

Humans are emotional creatures that learn new things and adopt new behaviors because they see practical reasons to. Rote memorization is more accurately thought of as training than as education. The instructor trains a large group[36] of students to parrot common English words and phrases. The students frequently don't even learn the meaning of the words they are saying or why each sentence they've memorized is structured the way it is. They are conditioned into voicing a certain series of sounds during particular social occurrences or in response to a different series of sounds being voiced to them. This is what conventional schooling institutions, by and large, call "learning English."

It usually goes that common vocabulary words come first, and then basic grammatical concepts. Finally, (if there's any time left) seemingly trivial aspects like pronunciation. Teaching vocabulary first is the fastest way to create the appearance of results. If your child can say some words and phrases in English, simple sentences like "Hello, how are you?" "I'm fine, thank you. And you?" "Where is the bathroom?" and so forth, it creates the appearance that they are communicating in English. In reality, they're just repeating sounds someone told them to memorize. Even if they do so accurately when prompted, it doesn't mean they are successfully cognizing the language. The evidence of this is that they cannot spontaneously use their memorized phrases correctly in contexts they have not already prepared for or subtly iterate upon them. They won't know how to say variations on their familiar phrases, such as "Hey, how are you feeling these days?" "I've been feeling a bit down, but things are getting better,"

---

[36] In my experience, up to 100 children can be packed into one public school English classroom at a time in countries facing overpopulation and/or bureaucratic mismanagement.

or "Are there any other bathrooms around here? That one is closed." They can only parrot what they've memorized, a combination of syllables that someone presented to them and that they might not even conceive of as separate words with their own meaning that can be reordered and transformed.

We use the verb "to parrot" for a reason. A parrot can speak, but it does not *know* how to speak. How can it do something it does not know how to do? Because it has been very well trained instead of educated. Education never means getting someone to the point where they can act in a superficially adequate manner. A dog, through repetition, can come to associate the English word "walk" and other tone-of-voice and body language indicators with the activity of going on an adventure outside with its owner. A cat can learn to correlate the sound of an electric can opener with the act of receiving precious wet food. But these are not examples of understanding. We train parrots, dogs, and other simple-minded animals.[37] We educate people.

The emphasis on entraining new action without education is most appropriate in skills requiring a specific type of physical dexterity and muscle memory to perform. Both can apply, of course. A musician must be trained to place their hands in a particular way on a musical instrument in addition to learning the structural rules that govern which notes to play. An athlete must train their body to kick, jump,

---

[37] There is an ongoing linguistic debate regarding intelligent non-human primates and their limited use of American Sign Language (ASL), such as the famous case of Koko the gorilla [Terrace, H. S., Petitto, L. A., Sanders, R. J., & Bever, T. G. (1979). Can an Ape Create a Sentence? *Science*, 206(4421), 891-902]. Detractors argue that apes show little to no grammatical understanding of the signs they associate with simple objects or actions. They cannot spontaneously morph words or construct sentences with complex, emergent meaning beyond that of what they have been explicitly trained with, even if they memorize hundreds of individual signs.

throw, catch, hit, or run while also studying the rules of the game that will determine good strategy and win conditions for their chosen sport. Similarly, a foreign language learner must learn how to use their mouth in unfamiliar ways to pronounce new sounds while also studying the rules of how that language works.

At the next level up from this style of animalistic behavioral reinforcement, we find the schools that bother to teach individual words to students (as both spoken sounds and written symbols), including their equivalent meaning in the students' native language. Now, at the very least, the students who memorize long lists of vocabulary can begin to conceptualize the world with some English terminology at the most basic level. They can look at a chair or a spoon and have the English word for it pop up somewhere on the screen of their mind, even if it is just as a possible alternative to the much more familiar native word for it.

With enough words memorized, they can begin to piece together an understanding of the most familiar parts of the world with English labels. They will hopefully be able to recognize most of these terms when used by English speakers, which means they will get a rough idea of what is being talked or written about. This will be true even if they fail to understand the structure of the sentence, several other key terms, and the relationship and importance of the few labels they do recognize. The world is slowly coming into focus in English, and functional fluency is within their grasp.

Acting on Learner Motivation

Learners who have practical purposes for learning new vocabulary are more likely to recall it. When you teach students English relevant to their interests and lifestyle activities, you minimize the additional work they must do to start thinking in English and incorporating English into their lives. English becomes an additional feature of something they've already decided to invest their time, thoughts, and emotions into. But when teachers force students to learn an arbitrary selection of English words and principles through exercises, they add to the work they must do. There is greater inertia to overcome because more has to change about how they think and act.

Under organic social conditions, people learn new words and structures because they find them useful or enjoyable. The effective English instructor cultivates conditions that enable that to happen for their students while sparing them the embarrassment, frustration, or miscommunication that might accompany making mistakes out in the real world. Passion, curiosity, fun, excitement, interest, and enthusiasm should characterize the dominant emotional experience of the English learning process. When we are enthused, we interact more vividly with our environment. We intake and process more information with fewer barriers to conception, integration, and later recall. This is especially true with skills we seek to make unconscious and effortless, such as communicating fluently in a foreign language. When learners can see both the short- and long-term benefits of acquiring fluent communication skills in English, they will cease to see the process as a chore forced upon them by authorities.

Activating this incentive gets easier as they get older. Teenagers and adults get better at projecting their long-term futures and devising realistic strategies than young children.

A child is more motivated by instant reward, which is emotional. Older learners can better apply their intellect and rational judgment to choose to subject themselves to something that might be momentarily dissatisfying but will pay dividends over the rest of their lives. They are better at weighing the equitability of delayed rewards.

When a student expresses something only because an authority figure commands them to or for wholly performative reasons, it is neither effortless nor authentic. The best a teacher can do is prompt and encourage students to express themselves in ways they know they need to focus on. Classroom prompting is always, to a degree, artificial, but it can approximate real-world use if the teacher is mindful of how they interject ideas to stimulate thinking in English. What is rarely attempted is tying the use of new words and grammatical principles to what the learner finds genuinely useful to think about and communicate.

Thought, unlike speech and writing, is hidden from external observation, making it difficult for English instructors to monitor and nurture its development. There is no way to look directly inside a learner's head and see how they perceive the world. You can only look at the tangible products of their thoughts and infer what is happening within. You can see the effort on their face and hear it in their voice if they struggle to find the words to describe things. It indicates that they probably first cognize things in their native language and translate them to English as they speak.

When English is used in the conventional EFL classroom, it is most often as manufactured speech about dull topics with predetermined vocabulary. "Where are you from? What's your favorite food or hobby? How many brothers and sisters do you have?" The reductive list of English communication options goes on. Organic English is not limited to manufactured small talk like this. It's about getting ideas people care about across to others so they can accomplish their important goals.

Every English speaker needs to start somewhere, of course. It's appropriate enough to begin the journey into English with direct translations of common phrases from the students' native language. That's one of the advantages of an adult learning a language over a child: They can compare new things they learn to old things they already know. But when a native speaker learns new words in their own language, it's most often because they're doing something or interacting with someone and hear or see a new word that describes something notably different than the words they're used to using. Through repeated exposure, context makes the new term's meaning clear. Rarely do they need an explicit definition of it unless it's an esoteric term with meaning not easily derived from context. The words that people remember and incorporate into their personal lexicons are ones they interact with often and offer new functionality.

Intermediate EFL students can already begin to do this when encountering new English words. Take the adjective "choppy" as an example. Some English students write in **choppy** sentences. A song playing on a radio station with bad reception will sound **choppy**. The smallest waves at the beach will break against the shore **choppily**. What makes this word easy to quickly derive the meaning of, remember, and incorporate into common use? Choppy sentences are sentences that are short and seem to end prematurely. Calling them choppy might be criticism and a suggestion that they should be longer and more complete. A choppy signal from a radio implies constant interruptions preventing a consistent broadcast from coming through. Choppy waves are in direct contrast to the long, full waves that are large enough for surfers to ride.

Why do we describe all these starkly different nouns (English sentences, radio signals, and ocean waves) as choppy? Because all of them, in our artistic interpretation, contain qualities of having been chopped. Something that should be large or complete has been broken up into smaller, incomplete pieces of the whole. They all contain the quality of choppiness, which is easy to immediately understand so long as you first know the verb "to chop" and have a basic grasp of common English suffixes and morphology. It's easy to remember and correctly apply the word "choppy" because the meaning is associated with a word the speaker likely already knows. They might even have a physical motion or image in mind (perhaps a karate-chopping arm or a large chef's knife coming down rapidly on raw vegetables) to make the meaning all the more visceral. What they should *not* do is rely exclusively on their native language's closest direct translation to retain its meaning.

The Necessity of Immersion

Long ago, in a Southern Californian high school, I studied Spanish because I was required to learn a foreign language for two years. I chose Spanish not because of any inherent interest in the language but because it seemed to be the path of least resistance. Spanish would be the easiest language to learn due to its similarities to English compared to languages with no shared root, alphabet, or grammatical conventions. And, living in San Diego, I was close to the Spanish-speaking country of Mexico. But as should come as no surprise, I learned little about practical Spanish use in those two years except a rudimentary vocabulary of common Spanish words and simple grammatical conjugations. I never put any of it into practical application outside the classroom, so I promptly forgot what little I had learned about Spanish.

Upon graduating, I went abroad to live in the Central American country of Costa Rica for a year. Though a fair amount of English is in active use there due to the large American and Canadian tourist and expat population, Spanish is the primary and official language spoken throughout the country. With no further Spanish study, aside from looking up the translations of new words as needed, I became conversationally fluent in Spanish under these conditions of natural Spanish immersion.

This situation of forced immersion worked so well because the general Costa Rican population was outgoing and eager to speak Spanish with a foreign tourist like me. Additionally, I dated and spent considerable time with a local woman who spoke only basic English. Communication in our relationship was difficult at the start. I had to struggle to use the little Spanish I knew to talk to her, and she had to struggle to use the little English she knew to talk to me. When I left the country, we were much more comfortable in each other's languages.

Several years later, I entered a relationship with a Ukrainian woman I met while traveling in Europe who already spoke good English. Because of her pre-existing English proficiency, we were able to communicate comfortably in my native language from the very beginning. This sounds like a good thing, but it made it all too easy for her to avoid ever using either of her native Russian or Ukrainian languages with me (neither of which I spoke).

My girlfriend, of course, appreciated the opportunity to practice and refine her use of English with a native speaker and teacher such as myself. But as I wanted it to be easier for us to communicate, I encouraged her to start speaking small amounts of Russian around me. My goal was to pick up on the sounds and patterns of Russian, just as I had with Spanish years before. And since I was an avid world traveler, I knew it would be useful to be conversationally fluent in another language used widely throughout Eastern Europe.

Surprisingly, getting my Ukrainian partner to use even the smallest amount of Russian with me proved nearly impossible. I thought I was being courteous by giving her permission to speak to me in a language she had been speaking all her life instead of English, a language she had more recently learned and still sometimes had trouble with. However, I found that if she tried to speak to me in Russian, she would have to stop and think about what she was saying and how easy it would be for me to understand it. She had never had to do this before because she had been speaking Russian all her life. She rarely consciously thought about how the language worked or how what she said would be understood by someone who didn't already know it.

With English, it was different. Because she had consciously learned the language as an adult, she was accustomed to planning out everything she would say. Her competence in Russian was still almost completely unconscious. That prevented her from using it, except in the rapid and unanalyzed way she did with other Russian speakers.

By the end of our two-year relationship, I had memorized by rote only one real Russian sentence: "Ya znayu, chto nichego ne znayu" (Я знаю, что ничего не знаю). It's the translation of a famous quote attributed to Socrates: "I know that I know nothing." I still, somewhat humorously, default to repeating it whenever someone asks me in Russian if I speak Russian. It's my way of saying that I only know enough Russian to say that I don't know Russian.

Later, I moved to the former Soviet republic of Armenia with hopes of learning the Armenian language through practical immersion with native Armenian speakers. There, I ran into a similar type of unconscious linguistic wall. My Armenian friends who already spoke English insisted on *only* speaking English with me. It was a rare chance for them to practice with a native speaker and improve based on my feedback about what they were doing wrong. It perplexed me how difficult it was to get almost any Armenians to speak Armenian with me. It didn't matter if it was a manufactured conversation for instruction or something spontaneous and functional out in the real world.

How Analysis Meets Intuition

When children first develop fluency in their native languages, intuition precedes analysis because the infant or toddler mind is not developed enough to rationalize things well. Children acquire language by constructing meaning from input and environmental association.[38] They hear sounds and see people talking. They come to associate certain sounds with certain objects, actions, and qualities. They even figure out that some sounds exist only to indicate relationships between other sounds. They can do all this without ever reading or writing a word or receiving a grammar lesson.

---

[38]   Tomasello, M. (2000). The item-based nature of children's early syntactic development. Trends in Sciences, 4(4), 156-163.

This intuitive approach from immersion takes them far enough to be able to understand basic information and communicate their fundamental needs. Analytical understanding becomes more useful when they are a bit older and are self-aware enough to consciously assess the linguistic knowledge they have so far taken for granted. Analysis refines the rough and vague into the neat and precise, enabling more effective communication when it is called for.

The adult foreign language learner has a distinct advantage over the infant, toddler, or child still adapting to their native language: Their rational faculties have already developed. That's why they can begin analyzing their target language before ever being immersed in it and forming intuitive associations. They need only basic exposure to the language's sounds and symbols to understand its organizational patterns (i.e., grammar). They can take this analytical study approach in tandem with forming intuitive associations through natural exposure, forming practical results more quickly than a child learning exclusively through immersion.

Of course, a child learning their native language still has a big advantage over an adult learning a foreign one. Because the child has not yet analytically studied a language and formed conscious associations with it, there is nothing to *unlearn*. An adult that has already analyzed a language will be accustomed to certain patterns of sounds, symbols, and grammatical constructions. With a foreign language sharing many of these aspects, the required adjustments might be small, such as with going from English to Spanish. Spanish uses the same Latin alphabet as English, though with the minor addition of the tilde (˜) as a special type of accent sometimes placed over the letter *n* (ñ) to change its pronunciation. The Spanish pronunciation of most letters will be similar to the most common English pronunciation in most cases (and remarkably more consistent).

The native English speaker is likely to only struggle with a few new sounds commonly used in Spanish but not included in English, such as the rolled "rr" sound[39] that involves the tip of the tongue vibrating ever-so-lightly against the roof of the mouth behind the front teeth. English doesn't use the tip of the tongue in the same ways Spanish does, so the mouth muscle memory of the English speaker is likely to make it difficult for them to pronounce these more delicate sounds correctly. They will default to the closest English approximation that they have already practiced.

Suppose the foreign language one is learning is radically different in writing, speech, and structure. It might feel like the learner has to forget virtually everything they know about how language should work. Any pre-existing habits and muscle memory will only get in the way. But even under these conditions, the right teacher can use the student's seemingly incompatible familiarity as a strategic reference. It just requires them to understand the differences between the two languages. "In your native language, you're used to constructing sentences in this way…" or "You pronounce the 'r' sound with your mouth like this…" followed by, "But try making these changes to that approach to end up with a closer approximation of how we learn to do it in our language."

Effective English teachers find the most appropriate blend of analysis (i.e., explicit explanations of how the language works) and intuition (i.e., exposure to organic use of the language). This gives each student the tools and examples to independently understand and use the language. This will

---

[39] Known by linguists as an alveolar trill.

be somewhat different for each student. They will all have their own cognitive temperaments. They will all have different levels of familiarity with English when they begin studying it. They will all come from native languages that vary in similarity to English. Effective English teachers are endlessly adaptable to all these nuances in the learning process.

Explicit explanations work better as corrections to mistakes after a student has reached a certain age and learned how to form English sentences through immersion and imitation. They do this primarily by listening to how other people communicate in English, not by having someone tell them what to do. Language learners copy what they hear and see other people doing first. This is how natural language acquisition always begins. Then explicit explanations help them refine their understanding and improve their mistakes. Conscious understanding can be built atop a foundation of good intuitive recognition.

Most native English speakers can use English grammar correctly nearly all of the time. However, few can explain explicitly why each grammatical choice is correct in each situation. They just know that that's how people around them do it and that it sounds wrong if they do it any other way. They know this because they've been hearing English used in certain ways for their entire lives. When something changes, it sounds different than what they're used to, and that's enough for most people to identify it as incorrect English. Accordingly, native English speakers are often least likely to notice errors in their own speaking/writing when those errors are so prevalent that seemingly everyone except English teachers and linguists is making them.

How we teach foreign English students is typically the opposite of this. That's why it's largely so ineffective at achieving conversational fluency. The people who become good at English are almost always either those who accidentally get exposed to the natural conditions under which languages are acquired or are so naturally passionate and autodidactic that they largely teach themselves. If EFL teachers want to play a more meaningful role in how learners acquire conversational fluency, they need to fundamentally change the way they assess and improve their abilities.

Explicit instruction and comparisons to the English learner's native tongue are most useful at the start of the learning process, particularly with older and more analytical learners. At this level, rote memorization of common words and phrases at least gives the budding learner some material to play with and experiment with manipulating. This ceases to be as useful once the learner knows enough English to communicate in a basic manner at the *intermediate* level. The middle stages consist predominantly of organically using English. The student reaches the point where they can organically form meaningful sentences independently instead of just repeating what they've memorized from others. Now, more progress will come from the student simply hearing the language and imitating it in conjunction with the explanations and translations already received.

At last, as the *advanced* English student approaches conversational fluency, explicit instruction again becomes useful for filling the holes and correcting the imperfections that remain. Now, they can, at last, formulate specific questions *in* English *about* English. They are ready to integrate the details and nuances that would have gone over their heads before. This is how they move beyond merely being understood by English speakers (despite their mistakes) to being perceived as something approximating a comfortable fluent speaker.

Advanced English speakers should have already given up their reliance on memorization and direct translation of words and phrases. They should be much better at inferring the meaning of unfamiliar terms through the context of what they understand. This is the same way native speakers predominantly grow their vocabulary too. Only in obscure situations do native speakers need to look up the meaning of a new word in a dictionary, which would be the equivalent of a foreign speaker looking up the translation of it back into their native language. Of course, they might also just want to verify the meaning of a particular word before using it in an official capacity for fear of being called out for a minor usage error. To a functional degree, everyone can understand more words than they can use with complete accuracy. We begin to use more specific or advanced terms when simpler alternatives are inadequate for what we wish to convey.

Consciously learning new words (covered in *Chapter 8: English Vocabulary*) is a useful but limited technique for English learners. It's how most language learners choose to start the learning process because it produces immediate results. For many of them, that's as far as the learning process goes. For more advanced students who might already have a functional grasp of grammar and the opportunity to apply what they know in real-world conditions, vocabulary is a good way to fill in the gaps in their communication ability. They can look up translations and commit them to memory whenever they struggle to communicate about an object or action they lack the appropriate word for.

However, this practical strategy is not the foundation for achieving English fluency. In conventional classroom settings, it only temporarily loads students with information to replicate when commanded. The memorized words are seldom applied as part of some kind of emergent linguistic structure (i.e., spontaneously forming complex sentences never heard or memorized due to an actual need to communicate a new idea). Memorizing English grammatical concepts (covered in *Chapter 7: English Grammar*) is certainly a step above memorizing mere words, but it, too, is typically quite limited in application.

Finally, we arrive at the most conceptually and mechanically simple aspect of English: pronunciation and spelling (covered in *Chapter 5: English Listening and Speaking* and *Chapter 6: English Reading and Writing*). Accordingly, it is also where pure rote memorization is most appropriate as a learning tactic. The basic rules of how phonemes and graphemes can be used to represent words can and should be trained, at first, in a controlled setting. Students need the most basic units of information to get traction in more advanced areas. Still, even regarding these simple aspects, EFL students will need to learn much like native speakers do—through organic immersion and practical use.

CHAPTER 4

LEARNER DIAGNOSIS AND TREATMENT

CONVENTIONAL EFL CURRICULUM is always generalized to address a range of students. The range varies from country to country and school district to school district. As such, standardized workbooks and lesson plans can only ever serve as a loose basis for learning English. They cannot ever optimally meet the needs of all students. Their content should be applied at the teacher's discretion for each student and situation because no two students have the same level of English proficiency or learning temperament when they begin their tutelage. Some will learn some things faster than others. This is of little consequence when teaching in a small group setting. But as classes grow, managing the variety in experience, ability, and interest becomes harder. It becomes helpful then to divide the learners into subgroups based on general understanding and learning preferences.

To discover how students best learn, there must be levels of interactivity not facilitated by the conventional EFL classroom. There cannot be an inordinately high ratio of students to teachers, or the teachers will be unable to give much individual attention to their students. They will be unable to adjust how they teach according to real-time feedback. Independent English instructors not beholden to conventional classroom standards are more empowered to set the terms of their classes and can limit the size or scope of what will be taught to not compromise the quality of instruction. EFL teachers must pay greater attention to find the strengths, weaknesses, and limitations of the English influences their students have been exposed to. A doctor must diagnose their patients before they can treat them, or they are just guessing what each patient needs according to general guidelines. English teachers should first do no harm.

But teachers made to operate under conventional restrictions will not take the time to see what their students already understand about English and what kinds of things they are in the habit of saying or writing. Dogmatists look for a grade, score, or accomplishment to indicate English ability. They fail to spot obvious holes and weaknesses in how students demonstrate what they can do in English. Even a factor as simple as the number of years already spent studying the language might be enough of a blanket indicator for an ineffective teacher to choose most of the learner's curriculum. Inevitably, when a student fails to conform to their teacher's generalized expectations, the blame is placed on the student. They treat the student as though they have done something wrong by not learning the right things at the right rate.

In even the most controlled of classroom settings, students will display a range of experience and ability in English. However, conventional classrooms tend to ignore the variation of students' learning experiences, preferences, and abilities (and even teachers' differing abilities to teach and engage students). It is in the interest of administrators for students to progress at the same speed, learn the same things, and pass the same tests, as it makes classroom management simpler and "progress" easier to measure.

A doctor does not operate this way. They don't blame the patient for not showing the right symptoms or improvement at an arbitrarily prescribed time. They adjust their treatment based on their unique problem, lifestyle, biochemistry, preferences, and the effectiveness of what has been tried so far.

The Dual-Teacher Approach

By combining a foreign native teacher with a local non-native one, students can get the best of both worlds in their English education. Local teachers will be better equipped to advise on certain aspects of the learning process than someone from a foreign country. They will hold greater empathy for students and have unique insights into the experience of learning English because they will have experienced the language learning process themselves under similar local conditions. The local teacher will better know what the students are learning in school and what their home life is like. They know what activities they will likely be busy with after school, how they communicate with their friends and family, or what opportunities they have to be exposed to English.

There will also be times when it is good to have the option of direct translation through the local teacher (though this should become less necessary as students get older and more skilled in English).

Having two teachers also makes classroom management much easier. It ensures students stay engaged in the lesson and that everyone participates and gets the specific help they need.

Finally, the dual-teacher approach can double as an internship or paid on-the-job training for teenagers and young adults already skilled in English and interested in becoming professional instructors. They will learn real-world class-room dynamics and teaching techniques likely not taught anywhere else in their country. At the same time, they will be learning the business and entrepreneurial aspects of being a teacher, the demand for which continues to grow. If they master these skills now, they could have EFL job security for life.

If the native EFL teacher has the ability and chooses to speak predominantly in their learners' native language, the learners will be tempted to respond in kind. Unconfident learners will only say in English whatever is easiest for them to say in English. They will omit many things that require more confidence and conscious effort to get across. A useful rule to implement then is that so long as English learners *can* say something in English, even if it takes effort, they should at least *attempt* to do so before defaulting to their native tongue. Even if they use a slightly wrong word... even if they mess up the grammar a bit... they should always attempt it. The goal is to make their thoughts as understandable as possible to English speakers. They should only switch back if they genuinely cannot find the right combination of words that mean a similar-enough thing in English. This will improve their ability to think spontaneously in English. They will grow more confident about trying, even when they might sound silly to native ears.

Instructions should only be translated into the learners' native language by the local teacher when necessary for ac-curate cognition. Use of the learners' native language should be minimized to the extent possible but not eliminated. Even then, the teacher can say what they mean first in English and then follow it up with a few clarifying words in the student's native language when it is clear that not everything said was understood as intended.

Learner Participation

The conventional EFL classroom is optimized for one-way, one-to-many interactions. A lone active teacher commands the attention of dozens of mostly passive learners. This authoritarian environment has nothing in common with the real-world conditions under which people organically acquire and use language.[40] Dozens of children sitting in rows at desks all day, writing and repeating information, only serves the function of making students easier to organize and control. Even having the teacher remain at the head of the class while students sit facing forward forces an unrealistic social hierarchy that is antithetical to inclusivity and participation. A more effective arrangement might be allowing the students to turn their desks or chairs toward one another in a circle to encourage group communication. That's more in line with how conversations occur out in the real world.

Shy students, in particular, are more encouraged to participate in a group they feel part of rather than as part of an anonymous unit being spoken to and taught at from afar. Conventional EFL makes introverted learners less prone to learning because they cannot comfortably express themselves under pressure.[41] One must use English to learn it, but

---

[40] If the social environment allows for it, a simple change in venue might be enough to make the English learning environment feel more real. Cafes, restaurants, parks, or shopping malls can all be effective locations for getting students to feel comfortable learning and implementing new aspects of English, so long as nothing in the environment prohibits focus and communication.

[41] Humor, for instance, can be a powerful social lubricant for breaking learners out of their shells. It makes heavy situations lighter and serious

many young learners will be reluctant to speak up until they are confident they can do so without mistakes. This is often a result of restrictive education policies that punish free expression, such as only allowing students to speak when spoken to. These students cannot resign themselves exclusively to reading, listening, and quiet self-study and get the full effects of English immersion.

English students are frequently afraid to look or sound stupid in front of a teacher (an authority figure) and each other (their peers). This leads to anxiety and interferes with learning. The effective English teacher must find a way to explain that everyone looks and sounds stupid the first time they try something new. The only way we get better is by not minding the fact that we don't sound perfect at the start of a new discipline. Only then can we gradually start to improve. Demonstrate to them, in whatever ways you can, that even you, the perceived authority figure, are willing to look and sound stupid, despite your skill and experience. Find something that even the weakest of your English students is demonstrably better at than you to show them that we are all strong or weak in our own ways. Demonstrate that you, too, are a fool in so many ways. Become the class jester. Are you a godawful singer? Belt a few lines like you're a few drinks into karaoke night. Let them see you be comfortable operating outside your element.

Perhaps the best demonstration of this is if you are still learning the students' native language and are just as bad at speaking it as they are at speaking English. It's a direct parallel that they will readily relate to.

---

topics easier to process. Chances are good that if you can get your shyest or least self-confident learners laughing and smiling, they will become more comfortable attempting to communicate with you in English.

Consider stage fright. If an English learner knows that someone will be evaluating every mistake in grammar, vocabulary, or pronunciation while they speak, they may get nervous about making simple errors that would otherwise not be an issue, such as if they were speaking to people who had only a similar level of limited proficiency. In many cultures, there is even a collective fear of speaking up or being noticed to exacerbate this problem. English teachers who encounter this problem should remind their students that the purpose of learning a language is to communicate. It's not about perfection except in the most formal of circumstances.

Communication is an attempt to transmit meaningful thoughts in one person's head to someone else's. Therefore, one of the best things teachers can do is first help learners understand their communication goals. Why do they want to learn English in the first place? Or are they only there at the behest of their parents or school? The student's self-chosen goals will create the context through which their budding knowledge of English should be applied and evaluated. It is an independent standard set by every student's internal motivators. It makes them responsible for how well they accomplish the goals they set for themselves.

For many students, your class may very well be the first time they've tried to speak English for practical communication or to express ideas and emotions spontaneously. They may have only ever had to use it during exams and in forced memorization exercises. That's why there can be a significant emotional barrier between what they have conceptually memorized and their ability to apply it. The effective teacher's duty is to find healthy ways to remove that barrier.

Using English Artificially

In any English setting, it is appropriate to begin instruction by surveying the students to learn why they want to learn English. This knowledge can inform how you will choose your curriculum and activities. The more teachers know about their students, the better they can prescribe the right "treatment" to help them achieve their goals. Even if this knowledge does not shape curriculum, it still helps the students stay motivated and engaged in the learning process. For some, it may be the first time they've ever thought of an authentic personal reason to study.

Since diagnosis requires a high degree of personalized interaction, it might seem antithetical to teaching English in large group settings. Effective English teachers find creative ways to structure their instruction to make the most of mixed age and proficiency levels, such as granting greater learner autonomy to help overcome differences in proficiency. The more practiced, developed, and outgoing students can be used as helpers and beacons to the rest. Structuring the English classroom this way also helps lessen the intimidating effects of one central authority figure reigning over everyone. The flawless native or fluent non-native teacher sets the template for English use that gets passed down to the more advanced students, who pass it along to the lesser-advanced ones. After learning, teaching others what they have already learned is the next logical step. It forces them to reconsider what they have unconsciously accepted and reframe it for minds that might work differently. Helping others learn English is the best English practice they can get.

Teaching offers a way of practicing English beyond repeating familiar linguistic concepts. It is active and targeted English for a purpose. It is real-time iteration, feedback, and adjustment. Explaining what you know to someone else is a powerful reinforcing tool.[42] The holes in your knowledge become apparent. True understanding entails rearranging the concepts you've accepted, making meaningful changes in your mind, and applying them in new contexts beyond what you've already tried. And since no two students learn best in an identical manner, the way to best teach to someone else might differ from how you learned it. The teacher-student relationship will be unique in each case.

English learners who teach also create more opportunities to practice their English because they will directly increase the number of people around them who speak English. The lack of other English speakers to talk to is a major obstacle to immersion in organic use. Most EFL students go home to families that don't speak English. They live in communities where hardly anyone speaks English. It's a network problem. You learn English to the extent that the other people around you speak English unless you are exceptionally motivated to reach beyond those limitations. Those who learn English before everyone around them are the early adopters of one of the most useful skills on the planet. They slowly influence others around them to approach their level.

At 17, one of my most promising English students had plateaued in her development via self-study. She could comfortably use English in casual real-world settings and consume popular English-language media. To break through her ceiling, she had to move away from being a mere user of

---

[42] According to Bloom's Taxonomy, there are six cognitive stages of learning in increasing stages of complexity and effect: remembering, understanding, applying, analyzing, evaluating, and creating. EFL learners who teach other students and discuss the process quickly move from the second stage of understanding all the way up to the fifth stage of evaluating by reflecting on how they themselves learned it and making adjustments for their own students.

English and become a conscious explainer of it to others. Explaining her knowledge of English to other students helped her stop thinking so much before speaking. It began to take less time for her to say things spontaneously. She began filling in the holes in her comfortable English knowledge and forced herself to expand beyond the common phrases she used in 90 percent of her English interactions. The experience inspired her to go into professional translation, which further improved her knowledge of the language beyond anything social interactions in her environment could offer. Now, instead of *paying* for (at best) minor improvement to her English, she was *getting paid* for improving her English far more effectively. Before teaching and translating, she had felt she was always guessing the best way to say something in English. She no longer questioned her unconscious knowledge of English. She felt more responsible for her words because she knew her example would set the template for others.

Often, the best English lesson is not even explicitly about learning English at all; it's about learning to do something new while using English. If you teach someone how to play the guitar, perform brain surgery, or throw a ball using English instructions, they're explicitly learning how to play the guitar, perform brain surgery, or throw a ball. But they will also be getting unconsciously better at English through exposure to common terms with clear context and meaning. What you teach could be almost anything you know how to do. It just has to be something your students have a genuine interest in learning and that you can explain in English terms they can mostly understand. It can even be something they already know how to do but have never thought about in English. It frames unfamiliar English terminology in activities they are already comfortable dealing with. The point is for learners to be emotionally engaged in what they're doing so that they see a practical need (and an emotional reward) for improving their English. The more English they can speak, the better questions they can ask their teacher, and the better they can begin to direct their learning. They can inform the teacher what they'd like to focus on learning next. Gaining access to a wider variety of educational opportunities is one of the most important reasons to learn English, after all. When they are ready, have them explain what they know so well to someone who doesn't know it using English; this will be the ultimate test of their comprehension.

Reinforcing English

When new information about the English language is introduced consciously, it needs to be reinforced with repeated use to simultaneously build intuitive associations.[43] It can be as simple as prompting the students with a question in English that uses the new vocabulary word or requires using the new grammatical principle. And then again, in a slightly different form. Iterate a few more times so that the context is always somewhat different and the meaning is thoroughly engrained.

However, outside of major cities, which usually have at least some international presence and amenities that cater to English speakers, there is often not enough English in practical use to acclimate to it. EFL teachers must encourage their

---

[43] According to linguistic behaviorism, language learning is primarily a process of habit formation and conditioning, similar to the way in which animals learn to respond to repeated stimuli through trial and error. Associations are reinforced through positive feedback and corrected through negative feedback.

students to find ways to supplement their English immersion outside of class at their discretion.

The ubiquitous presence of English-language media worldwide (often even in the most remote and underdeveloped places) comes to the rescue here. Our digital and globalized world presents countless opportunities for organic English exposure. Past generations were limited to the sparse and expensive English exposure offered by traveling to other countries or conversing with English-speaking foreigners in their own country. This is not the case anymore.

English learners everywhere can listen to popular songs in English. They can try to sing along. I'm frequently impressed by how students who can barely conjugate an English sentence when prompted to will be able to perform almost perfect word-for-word and note-for-note renditions of the current generation's favorite Western music. They don't fully grasp the meaning of every lyric analytically, but their emotional engagement and repeated exposure are enough to build intuitive understanding. This pop culture phenomenon allows for some convenient early lesson opportunities. The English teacher can help students analyze the lyrics of a song they already know and love, teaching them the meaning of the words they don't know and why the grammar works out the way it does. The only caveat is that songs are often written with copious use of slang, colloquialisms, poetic phrasing, and intentionally incorrect grammar to make them fit into the song's lyrical structure or poetic style. The teacher should be prepared to explain the use of non-standard English when it shows up in a song.

English learners can try to play online video games with strangers from beyond the sea. The mechanics of such games are usually designed to be simple enough to be accessible to a wide base of players. Once the student is engaged in the gameplay portion they can understand, they have a strong emotional incentive to try to understand in-game instructions or what other players say in text or voice chat. I'm often impressed by players communicating in English on game servers not located in parts of the world where I expect English to be the norm. It can be a virtual melting pot and is often beautiful to witness.[44] Strangers from different countries and cultures who would never have had any reason or opportunity to interact with each other and cooperate toward a shared goal learn enough of a globally shared language to engage in something they both care about.

Each video game has its own playstyle and win conditions, necessitating learning its terminology to communicate effectively within it. The context of one game might require students to understand and quickly implement simple tactical commands.[45] Failing to immediately understand or issue such commands (i.e., employ basic English fluency) normally means losing the game and facing social backlash from teammates and other in-game incentives to win. A different game might happen at a more leisurely pace with a casual setting that allows for idle conversation.[46]

---

[44] At least, it remains beautiful so long as no one gets frustrated enough to start calling other players "noobs," a crude gaming pejorative derived from the less offensive term "newbie," which itself is derived from "new player." However, even this colloquial insult affords students the opportunity to spontaneously learn new words from repeated real-world use in a specific cultural context.

[45] E.g., "There's a squad of enemies in the tower 100 meters to the north. They've got a sniper. Try to stun or flash them while I sneak behind for some easy kills. Hurry! Go now!"

[46] E.g., "Why did you choose the mage character class? I like the thief build because it lets me get more gold and loot faster. Do you have any good armor to trade?" It could even be something as grounded in real-world dynamics as "What country are you playing from? Let's try planting turnips in this part of our farm so we can sell them to the old man at the market in town and buy a bigger barn for our cows."

A single gaming match might only last a few minutes, and the team of strangers might never even learn each other's names or interact after that. Or their shared quest could take them on an adventure that lasts hours, necessitating more personal and complex levels of communication, perhaps even resulting in them befriending one another and choosing to go on more virtual adventures in the future. This is as close to real-world English social dynamics as one could hope for. Such opportunities will only increase as communication and gaming tech improve, such as with the recent advent of virtual reality and the metaverse. The modern EFL teacher would be negligent in ignoring these emergent English immersion opportunities.

English learners can, of course, also watch movies and television shows produced in English. For all its faults, Hollywood can be a great teacher. Certain movies and TV shows are prime candidates for entering the pop culture awareness of foreign countries, even those that don't speak English and for which no local language translation is available. I don't think I've ever been to a country where the show *Friends* or the *Star Wars* movies weren't known entities. English-language productions with international appeal often serve as people's first exposure to English and incentive to try to understand it. As a bonus, learners will probably have an easier time understanding the original English of a movie they have already heard or read the local dubbing or subtitles of. They will already have context for the words and foreknowledge of the events.

Making Corrections

In an ideal learning environment, teachers would be free to correct English learners the first time they see them make any errors in vocabulary, pronunciation, spelling, or grammar. The student would then retain the correct information and replace the incorrect information they had been working with. But every teacher knows that's now how error correction works in the real world. There is a limit to how effectively learners can adapt their working knowledge of something once it's been established. The longer they have been doing something wrong, the harder it is to start doing it right because errors become fossilized in the mind.[47] Conscious information goes to war with unconscious information. Habit takes time to break. What was learned must now be unlearned. We can keep only so many new rules in the working mind at any one time. Information should only be given at the rate at which it can be effectively integrated. For these reasons, effective EFL teachers should apply care and nuance in determining which errors to correct at an individual's stage of English development.

As a general rule, teachers should correct English errors when they know that the learner they are correcting should already know better—or when the error is so grievous that it significantly impedes communication. Using a somewhat less-than-optimal synonym for the ideal word is usually not a major hindrance to communication. Pronouncing one or two vowels incorrectly often leaves it obvious what word

---

[47] Fossilized errors are persistent errors that are difficult to correct even with extensive re-conditioning. Fossilization occurs when a learner consistently makes the same errors over time without correction so they become accepted as correct and deeply ingrained in their linguistic system. Even advanced English speakers can continue to make basic errors without realizing it.

the speaker is trying to say. A beginner student who speaks with a foreign accent can probably still be understood well enough to get basic ideas across. They should be commended for speaking at all despite their hampered execution.

Still, there are plenty of times when mispronouncing an *intended* word results in the correct pronunciation of an *unintended* word, which can lead to serious (and hilarious) communication problems. Smelling someone's *cologne* means something very different than smelling someone's *colon*. Ordering the *flaming yawn* at a nice restaurant will elicit a very different response from the waiter than ordering the *filet mignon*. We wash our hands with *soap* to eat *soup*, not the other way around. Slightly flubbing a grammatical construction usually still leaves the intended meaning of a sentence intact. Using the past simple tense when it would have been more appropriate to use the present perfect tense is often alright. Even native speakers do it. The fact that they even got the basis of their intended idea across to an English speaker is cause for celebration. But saying everything in the present simple tense because it's easiest for the student will surely lead to misunderstandings when the time someone took or will take place is significant to the intended meaning.

Advanced English students should be scrutinized through a finer filter than beginners. They are ready to refine their English to greater finesse and detail. Just getting the basic idea across isn't adequate anymore. There are areas of communication where even small miscommunications can have major effects. The more advanced the English learner, the more responsibility they should be willing to take for how their communications are received. In these cases, it is appropriate (perhaps imperative) for English teachers to interrupt and remind students of their quick, unconscious mistakes. While for more basic students, it makes sense to wait until the end of a communication to review what should have been said differently, advanced students will benefit even from what could otherwise be seen as a rude interruption as soon as a subtle mistake is heard—the type of mistake that only an attentive native speaker would even notice and that most would be too polite to bother pointing out. If the student is earnest in their desire to achieve conversational fluency, they should welcome these corrections, so long as they are given with respect and tact. Otherwise, they may get flustered, which can lead to a snowballing of mistakes that compound upon one another and cause a structural collapse of the learner's spontaneous self-expression. In the worst cases, it can even traumatize and discourage them from speaking English in front of an audience ever again.

Correcting English errors should always involve demonstrations of the correct way to say the word or phrase in question and a suitable explanation of why it is correct. The teacher should also explain to the extent that the student can understand why the correction matters and how it contributes to better communication. People are much more likely to retain information when they understand why it is correct and the practical utility of rectification.

EFL learners must also realize that mistakes are normal, accepted, and the best way to improve. One possible way to do this is to involve the students themselves in the process of giving corrections. Make a game out of it. See who in the class can catch the most mistakes made by their classmates (so long as they are mistakes that the students should have known by now not to make). It encourages everyone to listen more intently to how their peers speak and reflect on their normally unconscious habits.

CHAPTER 5

ENGLISH LISTENING AND SPEAKING

CONVENTIONAL EFL OFTEN treats pronunciation as a superfluous aspect of learning the language—as if having a good accent and being well-understood in speech were merely an aesthetic flourish. English learners should be free to mostly ignore it during their language acquisition, so they seem to think. It's window dressing atop a large English vocabulary. But pronunciation is vastly more important than EFL educators typically give it credit for, as the sounds native English speakers use in their speech form the base units of information in the learner's ear and mind.

Pronunciation and spelling are analogous as base units; learning pronunciation if you want to speak is equivalent to learning the alphabet if you want to read. Pronunciation addresses how to make the sounds required for spoken English, and spelling addresses how to write the symbols required for written English. If there are some sounds you cannot identify or replicate with your own pronunciation, it's like learning only part of the alphabet. Imagine trying to read a language that way. You'd be trying to fill in the blanks constantly. Your brain wouldn't be able to remember it all or make sense of it quickly. Half of the map would be missing. If you try to learn a language with sounds you're not used to, you won't remember the words that use those sounds very well. It will difficult to construct meaningful sentences and express them without conscious effort.

Accent also has an enormous effect on the presentation elements of speaking English. If uncommon constructions are delivered with enough confidence, listeners will be more likely to accept them as valid because they will perceive them as intentional instead of as signs of linguistic incompetence. They will think there must be some important reason that the speaker chose an odd phrasing or an original way to emphasize something when there were easier, more common options. There must be some subtle meaning they intended that would not have been connotated by the standard option for describing what they are talking about. When an English speaker sounds unconfident or speaks with a heavy foreign accent, listeners might assume the speaker does not know any better. This will remain true no matter how technically correct the construction can be argued to be.

Even among native English speakers from the same country, there can be an enormous variety in standard, acceptable, and understandable pronunciation. An American raised on the coast of Southern California, where people might speak with a stereotypical surfer bro or gnarly chick accent and dialect,[48] will sound different than one raised in Texas or Oklahoma who speaks with a Western "cowboy" accent.[49] A cockney Londoner[50] has noticeably different pronunciation than a kilt-wearing bagpipe-playing Scot.[51] Even though they all

---

[48]   Think Keanu Reeves' laid-back portrayal of Ted Theodore Logan in 1989's *Bill & Ted's Excellent Adventure* and its sequels or Sean Penn's iconic Jeff Spicoli in 1982's *Fast Times at Ridgemont High*.

[49]   Think John-Wayne- or Roy-Rogers-esque yippee-ki-yaying, git-along-little-dogieing diehard good old boys.

[50]   Think actors Michael Caine's or Bob Hoskin's distinctive voices.

[51]   Think Ewan McGregor's portrayal of Mark Renton in 1996's *Trainspotting* or Mike Myers' Shrek in 2001's *Shrek* and its sequels.

speak English, it may still be nearly as difficult to understand one another as if they were speaking different languages. How can we rightfully call any of these manners of native English pronunciation more "correct" than any other or, for that matter, any non-native accents and English pronunciation quirks that show up in other parts of the world that adopt English?

The answer, as always, lies with how well a speaker's pronunciation aids them in their goals as a communicator. What manner of pronouncing English will make the learner be understood as best as possible by the English speakers (whether native or non-native) they wish to be understood by? A thick non-native accent might not impede communication if the learner only communicates in English with others with the same accent. It might, however, become a major obstacle if they talk to English speakers across the globe with widely differing ways of enunciating based on where they are from. It obviously diminishes English's role as a global lingua franca if it can only be spoken effectively in specific regional settings. "Good" English pronunciation, therefore, is that which can be widely understood as clear English with minimal effort or confusion by listeners.[52]

---

[52] As noted, Standard American English pronunciation seems to have emerged as the global ideal in most places outside of Europe. Whether this is due to it having phonetic qualities that make it inherently easier to understand or due to Western media exposure is, more or less, irrelevant. More often than not, foreign learners will tell me that my American pronunciation of English is clearer than other English accents they are exposed to.

Listening Naturally Precedes Reading

Except with older students who have developed a specific aptitude and preference for written language, listening is a more natural method of intaking the basic information of English. New learners cannot help but start to decipher its common phonetics when repeatedly hearing them, even if they are not consciously trying to. Even foreign learners who have never taken an English lesson may have heard the sounds of English throughout their lives, giving them a major starting advantage. Listening and speaking skills eventually lead to developing reading and writing skills.

That is why even native English speakers with excellent diction still need to speak slowly and clearly around foreign learners. It is also why non-native English teachers should work to make their accent sound as clearly intelligible to native speakers as possible. EFL teachers will be the primary influence on how learners adapt to the phonetic components of English and begin to form their own accents. Non-native EFL teachers frequently cannot produce the essential phonemes of English correctly, so how can they teach them to others? How can they correctly influence their students to start replicating what they hear if what they hear is wrong? It's a vicious cycle of poor imitation.

Their challenge is fixing the mistakes made during their own foreign English education long ago, which in many ways means returning to the beginning. Most are not humble enough to attempt this. It's like willingly becoming a baby again and learning to talk for the first time, exposing themselves to the correct sounds of English and earnestly trying to replicate them. They're probably going to look and sound dumb while they do this because it means going back to the babytalk stage of English. They have to accept that the way they have been using their mouth to make sounds in English has been inadequate. They need to learn to use their entire vocal apparatus in new ways. They need to practice moving their lips, teeth, throat, and tongue differently, which will sound and feel awkward for a while.

Muscles learn through repetitive action. Muscle memory means we are more inclined to repeat a familiar series of actions and move within a familiar range, which only gets more reinforced the more we do it. The earlier we start training ourselves to use our mouth muscles to sound how we are supposed to in English, the easier it will be to retain that muscle memory for life. The longer we spend pronouncing things incorrectly, the harder it will be to retrain ourselves.

Good pronunciation starts with recognizing the foreign sounds you are exposed to, which is much easier if you're young when you first hear them. So too, will be replicating them with your own vocal apparatus. It's harder to learn precise auditory differentiation and muscular control later on when you're already used to hearing and speaking only a limited range of other sounds required by your native language. That's why recognizable foreign accents exist and are specific to different regions. The ear and mouth have been trained in particular ways across different places.

Infants and toddlers naturally attempt to replicate the phonemes they hear in their social environments, even without assigning any cognitive meaning to particular arrangements of those phonemes as words, let alone arranging those words into specific sentences with more complex emergent meanings.[53] Foreign English-learning adults would do well to emulate toddlers in this regard.

---

[53] The imitation theory of language acquisition proposes that babies and toddlers learn to produce and differentiate speech by imitating the

The Long and Short of English Vowels

What is a vowel? It's a sound produced by the vocal cords with an open vocal tract. The placement of the tongue and rounding of the lips subtly influence the sound that comes out. These physical differences can be so subtle that it's hard to even describe them physically. To make matters worse, native English speakers can be quite inconsistent about vowel pronunciation. The inconsistency makes it harder to remember which letters might be needed in certain common words when trying to spell them or which sounds to make when pronouncing written words.

We broadly categorize vowels into two categories: long and short.[54] The easiest way to tell the difference is that long vowel sounds are felt at the top of the mouth (with the mouth more closed), and short ones are felt at the bottom (with the mouth more open).[55] There's a reason that the dentist will tell you to open wide and say "ahhhhhhhh" with the short "o" (/ɑ/) sound instead of the long one; it requires you to open your mouth more.

The easiest way for a foreign learner to conceive of the primary vowel sounds in English is to think of the five letters we primarily use as vowels (*a, e, i, o,* and *u*). Each has a long and short sound associated with it, making ten in total. The

---

sounds they hear from their primary caregivers, which allows them to gradually build up a working vocabulary of words and phrases. This process is driven by the brain's natural ability to detect patterns and make connections between sounds and meaning.

[54] All short vowel sounds technically have to end with a consonant sound. If we end a word with them, we subtly add the "h" (/h/) sound to bring them to a close. Only long vowel sounds can be voiced purely on their own.

[55] Perhaps better names for them would be top and bottom vowels, as the length for which you can hold them has nothing to do with their pronunciation.

long vowel sounds are easier for foreign learners to remember because they are essentially just the name of the letter they are associated with.

The long "a" (/eɪ/) in "hate" sounds like the name of the letter *a*.

The long "e" (/i/) in "Pete" sounds like the name of the letter *e*.

The long "i" (/aɪ/) in "bite" sounds like the name of the letter *i*.

The long "o" (/o/) in "hope" sounds like the name of the letter *o*.

The long "u" (/u/) in "tube" sounds like the name of the letter *u* (minus the unwritten "y" (/j/) consonant sound it starts with).

These are typically the easiest for foreign learners to remember and pronounce correctly. They tend to have more trouble differentiating and remembering the short vowel sounds.

The "a" (/æ/) sound in "hat" is short.

The "e" (/ɛ/) sound in "pet" is short.

The "i" (/ɪ/) sound in "bit" is short.

The "o" (/ɑ/) sound in "hop" is short.

The "u" (/ʌ/) sound in "tub" is short.

Conveniently, each of these long and short vowels descends further down in the mouth as you pronounce them alphabetically. Try it with the long vowels first. Say, "hate Pete bite hope tube." Now just "ate ete ite ope ube." Then just the long "a e i o u" sounds as quickly as you can. Feel how the vowels get lower in your mouth as you go.

Now do the same with the short vowel sounds. Say, "hat pet bit hop tub." Now just "at et it op ub." Then just the short "a e i o u" sounds as quickly as possible. The same descending pattern occurs.

There are, of course, technically more vowel sounds in English than just the ten listed here. The long "ow" (/aʊ/) sound in "pout" goes even lower than the long "u" (/u/) in "tube." Its corresponding short "ow" (/ʊ/) sound in "put" goes even lower than the short "u" (/ʌ/) in "tub." But these ten, as delineated into five top and five bottom sounds that can easily be mapped onto the five vowels, serve as an excellent starting point for foreign cognition and pronunciation.

As with all other aspects of English pronunciation, learners' difficulties depend primarily on what sounds they are used to using in their own language. The sounds that are easy for students from one part of the world might be difficult for those from another.[56]

English, like every other language, has fewer vowels than consonants. This is due to the natural limitations in our vocal apparatus to produce the sounds defined as vowels (i.e., an open vocal tract). There are far more possible combined uses of the lips, teeth, and tongue to produce more consonants with a closed vocal tract. You can't even smoothly transition between most consonant sounds because they require too big a change in the arrangement of the vocal apparatus. That's not an issue with vowel sounds because you are only vocalizing with your throat and subtly changing the open placement of the mouth to produce a different vowel. You can easily fuse two of them into diphthongs, which are often difficult to distinguish between monophthongs because of how smooth

---

[56] The vowel sound I've heard foreign English learners consistently have the most trouble with is the short "i" sound (/ɪ/). Interestingly, it's usually easier for them to pronounce it as part of a short word or sentence like "this is sick," which features three short "i" sounds followed by consonants in a row, than on its own as an isolated vowel sound.

the transition between subtly different mouth placements and the similar vowel sounds they create can be.[57]

Confused Consonants

While vowels can easily be confused for one another because of subtle differences between them in sound and mouth configuration, consonants tend to be strikingly different. There is much greater variety in what we have to do to say them and how they sound. Because of this naturally great variety, foreign English learners can be confused by novel consonant sounds that seem normal to native ears.

The sounds for "l" (/l/) and "r" (/ɹ/) are liable to be mixed up by non-native English speakers in certain parts of Asia. The English "l" sound either does not exist. Only an approximation requiring a different tongue position does. They might tend to default to the "r" sound instead because it is the closest in physical pronunciation that they are used to. The only physiological difference between the "l" and "r" sounds is that the "l" requires a slight extension of the tip of the tongue to meet the inside of the front teeth. Yet, even this tiny difference is enough to conflict with the engrained muscle memory of populations who have never had to position their mouth that way to make that sound before.

The English "w" (/w/) and "v" (/v/) sounds are subject to similar befuddling, particularly in Russia and other parts of Eastern Europe that speak Slavic languages. The "w" sound isn't in native use there, so the closest approximation is to extend the top front teeth over the bottom lip to make a "v"

---

57   As noted in their International Phonetic Alphabet (IPA) symbols, even the seemingly singular long "a" (/eɪ/) and "i" (/aɪ/) sounds are actually combinations of two vowels each (the latter of which is the short "i" sound (/ɪ/) in both cases) when conventionally pronounced.

sound. The "w" sound requires rounding the lips instead, which they simply aren't accustomed to doing.

Similarly, the "s" (/s/), "sh" (/ʃ/), "th" (/θ/ or /ð/), and "z" (/z/) sounds can be notoriously difficult for foreign learners to get right, as each requires only minute changes in the positioning of the teeth and tongue or the subtle addition of voicing by vibrating the vocal folds.

How you teach pronunciation of the most difficult English consonants will be influenced by what part of the world you are in and what your students have the most difficulty adapting to. As well, students conceive of pronunciation best in different ways.[58] Those with naturally good ears and musical minds might easily differentiate between the sounds they need to learn. Others with more kinesthetic awareness and control over their bodies might be better off conceptualizing and feeling the difference in how the parts of the mouth and throat move.[59]

The effective English teacher recognizes that a language can be conceptualized through many equally valid filters and that students have their own strengths and preferences for

---

[58] Howard Gardner's theory of multiple intelligences proposes that individuals excel to different degrees with different types of intelligence or ways of intaking and processing information, such as linguistic, logical-mathematical, spatial, bodily-kinesthetic, and musical. Learners with high spatial intelligence, for instance, may benefit more from visual diagrams and maps to vocabulary and grammar than from a heavy emphasis on phonetic imitation. Trying to make all learners conform to the same methods of input and understanding would disadvantage many of them.

[59] Precise placement of the lips, teeth, and tip of the tongue at the front of the mouth are easier for a learner to see and for a teacher to articulate than changes that take place in the back of the mouth or throat. Guttural throat sounds have to be reverse-engineered from how they sound instead of by copying how they look to make. In my own experience, it's easier to learn languages with phonemes that emphasize tip-of-the-tongue placement than guttural throat use simply because the learner has an easier time seeing what is happening to make the required sounds.

approaching it. We should all be willing to adapt to the needs of each student to the best of our ability if we ever want to see them making meaningful progress toward something approximating native English pronunciation.

Intonation Across Sentences and Time

There are small inflective changes that we apply to individual syllables within words, and there are tonal changes we apply across words in a sentence to influence how the sentence as a whole is perceived. Intonation even applies on a broader scale across whole paragraphs and long-form speeches that can go on for several minutes. What this means is that when a native English speaker speaks, the beginnings of their sentences usually sound different than the ends. As well, the important parts get naturally emphasized throughout the sentence. The speaker's emotional state becomes clear to anyone who listens, and it changes the connotative meaning of the words they are saying. These tonal changes are subtle and automatic for native speakers. They rarely even think about them. It's just all part of the natural flow of an English sentence or sequence of sentences.

The voice a native English speaker uses to tell a friend that their grandmother just died is not the same one they would use to tell the world they just won the lottery or the same one they would use to insult someone they hate. There are clear differences in tone. The foreign English learner is likely to limit their English expressions to a narrower range of intonation. They are not practiced enough in pronouncing the sounds of English to naturally change their voice to match the intended or appropriate emotional context.

That's part of why we think robots are so, well, "robotic" when they speak. There is something clearly inhuman about them, and most of it is owed to the fact that they have a narrow and artificial range of emoting. They don't have the same natural intonation we expect from humans.[60] Have you ever called an automated customer service line that forms messages out of pre-recorded words? Those words are recorded individually without the proper intonation as determined by how they will be used in each new sentence. The patchwork sentences sound strange to human ears. You have to focus harder on what is being said because you have no intonation clues from which to determine the subtle meaning. Each syllable might be perfect in isolation but lack emergent tonal qualities in sequence. The whole is less than the sum of its parts.

Emotions give context to word choices. Saying, "I broke your computer," with an angry emotional context means something completely different than saying, "I broke your computer," with a guilty or sympathetic emotional context. There's an implied meaning in tone of voice that doesn't have to be explicitly verbalized. In fact, much of the communication we do is not explicit. It's implied by what we don't say, how we say things, the context in which we're speaking, how we're physically gesturing, etc. If a foreign English speaker has a great vocabulary and perfect grammar but doesn't know how to use emotional inflection when they speak, they risk being misinterpreted and misunderstood. Yet, conventional foreign English education frequently downplays this

---

[60] Range of emotion isn't just limited to speech. A robot's face, even if we can make it look human, still struggles to copy natural human facial expressions in a convincing manner at our present state of robotics technology.

aspect of communication in English or completely overlooks it.

What is the difference between singing and talking? How does it affect communication? What additional qualities does singing typically have that talking does not? Singing is an extremely heightened form of emotional inflection. That's why a character in a musical has to sing what they mean to convey instead of just saying it and why they even might start moving their whole body around in time with what they're singing as part of an emotive dance. Merely saying the words would not convey all the emotion they intend. Even shouting them would not.

Unconfident EFL learners won't have nearly as much inflection and emotional sensitivity in the tone of their words. They will use a muted, monotone, and simplified way of speaking if they are worried about saying words in the wrong way (on top of their base concern about even using the right words in the first place). They will have to grow more comfortable emoting naturally in English.

Consequently, the foreign English learner won't be able to cognize whole sentences in English at first. They will only pick up on the words they recognize and try to guess the context of what is being communicated and the meaning of the words they don't know. But they will not recognize an English sentence as a complete unit of thought yet. It's partially about the foreign syntax; the order in which the words are being said might differ from what they're used to. It also has to do with how the English speaker inflects their sentences in ways the foreign listener is not accustomed to. Their mind is not processing the beginning of a thought as the beginning, the middle as the middle, and the end as the end. It's just word, word, word, word, and word.

Foreign English learners who want to improve their accents and intonation should find examples of what they consider to be good, clear, native English speakers that they can understand easily and try to imitate or mirror them.[61] They won't sound exactly like the influences they've chosen, and they shouldn't try to. They should try to sound like themselves with an approximation of the other person's accent. Emulating someone else's manner of speaking English is like singing another person's song. No matter how talented they are, few singers will ever sound anything like Whitney Houston when they belt out the chorus of her hit song *I Will Always Love You*.[62] You can probably already hear a horrendous karaoke version of it in your head: *"Annnndd IIIIIIIIIIIIIIIIIIIII-eeeee-IIIIIIIIIIII will aaaaalways loooooooooove youuuuuuuuuuuuuu-eeeeee-uuuuuuuuuu."*

It's not just because she sings difficult songs and you have to be a good singer even to hit the notes in her melodies. It's that few people's voices sound like Houston's. Her timbre is unique. If another singer tries to alter their natural voice to sound exactly like her, it will most likely come across as forced and ridiculous. A good singer, unless their goal is to do a perfect celebrity impression, should try to sound like themselves hitting the same notes and singing in a similar style to Whitney Houston.

---

61 Professionally produced audiobooks are great sources from which to emulate native English pronunciation and accent. While any type of native English media can help with general exposure, audiobooks are intentionally narrated in a clear tone and at a pace slower and more measured than spontaneous real-world speech. It's literally a narrator's job to speak in a clear and appealing way, so who better to emulate?

62 Though popularized by Whitney Houston's signature rendition of it for the 1992 movie *The Bodyguard*, the original song was released by Dolly Parton in 1974.

It is the same when the foreign English speaker first attempts to copy an English speaker's accent that differs from their natural way of speaking. They should aim to discover how their voice will sound once they acclimate to the English language's phonetic range and intonation patterns. This takes an enormous amount of confidence that most new English speakers simply don't have. It's like putting on a performance. At first, your new English voice feels like a false pretense to you, like you are pretending to be someone else. You will have to put extra conscious attention to it. But after a while, it becomes unconscious and natural.

One non-native teaching assistant I worked with was a young woman who had learned English under wide-ranging real-world conditions that exposed her to various accents from India, America, England, and parts of East Asia. The result was that her accent in English sounded utterly distinct from that of all other English speakers in her country. It was a subtle blend of many ways of emphasizing syllables in words and words in sentences that didn't sound like it could have come from any single part of the world. And though her pronunciation certainly didn't sound like what native English speakers are used to hearing, it also lacked the clunkiness, uncertainty, and high conscious effort associated with most non-native speakers. Her one-of-a-kind accent came across as more of a personal affectation than a hindrance to her communication, as though her personal style was deliberately put on display when she spoke. That's a standard that all non-native English speakers can aspire to without trying to force themselves to sound flawlessly British, American, Australian, or Canadian.

CHAPTER 6

ENGLISH READING AND WRITING

THE INVENTION OF the printing press in the 15th century was revolutionary because it enabled the scaling of access to information that had previously been confined to oral recitation or painstaking manually written reproductions. In recent centuries, written information has at last become affordable and accessible to ordinary people. Therefore, the incentive to learn to read has risen too. Those who cannot read cannot reap the rewards of directly accessing the abundance of written information now available worldwide.

In fact, literacy rate is considered one of the key human development metrics worldwide by organizations like the United Nations Development Programme (UNDP)[63] and The World Bank[64] to indicate potential for economic growth, poverty reduction, and social development. The ability to read opens up a world of inexpensive information. Those who can read can go on to acquire useful skills and produce and consume countless things of tangible value that would otherwise have been beyond their reach. All other things being equal, standard of living correlates with literacy.

---

[63] https://hdr.undp.org/data-center/human-development-index#/indicies/ HDI

[64] https://genderdata.worldbank.org/indicators/se-adt/

The merits of general literacy apply to an even further extent to English literacy. Those who cannot read and write in English are disadvantaged in a world abundant with information published in English. We must include good English reading and writing skills under the umbrella goal of conversational English fluency. We must consider how spreading English literacy to places where it is scarce could vastly improve the general quality of life.

However, the spread of English literacy presents a unique problem that learning to read in most other languages does not. It is not just foreign learners of English who struggle with learning to read it. Even native English-speaking children learning to read for the first time will consistently take longer than children in similar positions with their own native languages. Children from most European countries, for instance, approach complete accuracy in reading their native languages at a foundational level by the end of first grade. The major exception is English speakers, who need a few more years to approach complete accuracy in reading and writing.

Where there is a consistent one-to-one relationship between letters and sounds, children tend to learn to read more quickly and accurately than with languages with more complex orthographies.[65] This is a luxury English lacks. Because of its alphabetic inconsistencies, English spelling can seem chaotic beyond comprehension. Spelling bees and contests that reward English speakers for their ability to remember how to spell even common words should be proof of this.

Still, calling English spelling nonsensical is an oversimplification. Native English speakers can encounter a variety of

---

[65] Seymour, P., Aro, M., & Erskine, J. (2003). Foundation literacy acquisition in European orthographies. The British Journal of Psychology.

new words in writing and approximate how they ought to be pronounced or infer their most likely spelling when hearing them spoken aloud. This could not be the case unless there was some underlying order to the chaos and some meaning behind the apparent madness of the English alphabet.

Mapping Letters and Sounds

The simplest written languages are designed with a one-to-one correspondence between written symbols (graphemes) and spoken sounds (phonemes). In such a language, any given letter is pronounced the same way every time it is encountered in a word, and there are no redundancies between multiple letters that can represent the same sound (or vice versa). Prominent alphabetical languages largely work this way, with some notable and easy-to-remember exceptions. Occasionally, a letter might change or omit its pronunciation depending on the context in which it is used. Multiple letters used in sequence might also take on a new emergent pronunciation unrelated to the individual sounds.

More than any other common written language, English fails to adhere to a consistent one-to-one mapping between its letters and sounds, so it can be difficult for foreign learners to read it. The Latin alphabet English uses has only 26 letters to represent the more than 40 distinct sounds in speech. Many of the 26 individual letters can be pronounced in more than one way, and that's *before* combining them with other letters as part of some emergent rule. Reading letter combinations correctly often depends on the context of the word we are trying to decipher. The letter combination *ch* can be pronounced in at least three different ways without breaking any rules.[66] All in all, more than 200 possible letter combinations form just 44 sounds in English.

The Spanish language is a great example that uses the same Latin written alphabet as English but with simpler and more consistent pronunciation for each letter. One of the few well-known exceptions is what happens when the letter *l* is doubled. A singular Spanish *l* is pronounced the same as the standard English variant (/l/), as in "like," "lemon," or "limousine." A doubled *ll* is pronounced like the standard English letter *y* (/j/), as in "your," "yellow," or "yesterday," in most dialects of Spanish. This is as arbitrary as the common English digraph *ph* being pronounced like "f" (/f/) in English. Americans who don't speak even conversational Spanish but love Mexican food will know how to pronounce "quesadilla" correctly, with "ya" (/jə/) as the final syllable instead of "la" (/lə/). Spanish remains easy to read because this is one of only a few emergent rules that go beyond its one-to-one letter-to-sound alphabet, and this rule is applied consistently.

The Americans who know this correct pronunciation, more often than not, learn it through the repetition of contextual clues. An American is likely to hear the word "quesadilla" spoken aloud many times before they see it in writing, so they will have already ingrained the "ya" pronunciation in their mind and can easily affix it to the written word when they see it. Native English speakers are used to this because their language has many changing rules and inconsistencies. How do you know how to pronounce the name of the famous Edgar Allan Poe story, *The Cask of Amontillado*? Amontillado is a Spanish variety of wine. But you don't need to know that.

---

[66] The words "**ch**rome" (/k/), "**ch**eer" (/tʃ/), and "**ch**ef" (/ʃ/) all use ch to make distinct sounds but can be easily read and pronounced by native English speakers.

You just need to have heard the name of this famous story mentioned before or have already gotten accustomed to the *ll* = "y" pronunciation pattern from exposure to other Spanish-looking or Spanish-sounding words.

English is neither simple in translating from sound to symbol nor from symbol to sound. The long "e" (/i/) vowel sound has ten possible spellings in common use. It can be made with combinations of *e, ea, ee, ei, ey, e_e, i, ie, i_e,* and *y*.[67] Similarly, the words "**oh**," "sh**ow**," "g**oat**," "th**ough**," "ph**o**ne," and "plat**eau**" all use different combinations of letters to produce the same long "o" (/o/) vowel sound. Moving in the opposite direction, the same combination of letters can have more than one sound associated with it. The *ough* combination of letters can be pronounced as at least five different vowels. They can be understood thr**ough**[68] t**ough**[69] thor**ough**[70] th**ough**t,[71] th**ough**.[72] How is the foreign learner supposed to derive the correct way to read or spell such words if they lack familiarity with the conventions of English? It cannot be done by knowledge of individual letters alone.

Reading from Letter Combinations

No native English speaker learns how to use the alphabet from the ground up. Counter-intuitively, their ability to read is not the direct consequence of learning how to use the alphabet. Children learn to read and spell English simultane-

---

[67] E.g., be, seat, free, deceive, key, meme, studio, relieve, marine, and baby.

[68] long "u" (/u/)

[69] short "u" (/ʌ/)

[70] long "o" (/o/)

[71] short "o" (/ɔ/)

[72] Long "o" again. The fifth vowel not listed in this phonetically ridiculous sentence is the long "ow" (/aʊ/) sound, as in "pl**ough**."

ously.[73] Yes, they may memorize the alphabet song, just as the children of native speakers of other languages often memorize their own songs designed to help them learn their alphabets. But the ability to read and write in English also comes from exposure to various words with mixed spelling conventions. The human brain is a pattern-seeking machine. It notices when certain bits of information are lumped together frequently. From that, it begins to discern what new data bits would most appropriately be lumped together. Every native English speaker can spot when a word doesn't look like it belongs among the established patterns of the language.

There's a popular linguistic meme that captures this phenomenon. You may have seen it or something like it.

If *gh* can stand for *p* in "hiccough,"

If *ough* can stand for *o* in "dough,"

If *phth* can stand for *t* in "phthisis,"

If *eigh* can stand for *a* in "neighbor,"

If *tte* can stand for *t* in "gazette,"

And if *eau* can stand for *o* in "plateau,"

Then the way to spell "potato" could be *ghoughphtheight-teeau.*

The meme's point is to mock the seemingly absurd ways we often spell things in English. It takes the worst of these individual practices to what appears to be a logical extreme. And indeed, a foreign English student might accept this spelling as a legitimate possibility because it breaks no explicit rules they can identify. However, the joke of this meme ignores the fact that native English speakers would never come

---

[73] Ehri, L. C. (1997). Learning to read and learning to spell are one and the same, almost. In J. Downing & S. D. Twombly (Eds.), Critical issues in early literacy: Research and pedagogy (pp. 49-73).

across the word "ghoughphtheightteeau" and accept it as valid English, and certainly not that it should be pronounced as "potato" (/pə'teɪtoʊ/), even if they couldn't explain to you exactly why. If they tried to pronounce it, it would probably sound more like "gof-theto" (/gɒf-θɛtoʊ/) or "goft-height-o" (/gɒft-haɪt-oʊ/).

This absurdly spelled word relies on borrowing spelling practices from multiple incompatible languages and placing them in an order that doesn't make any sense. The spelling of "hiccough" is an anomaly. It resulted from an association in the 1600s that the act was related to coughing. The standard "hiccup" spelling has mostly replaced it. There is no other established pattern for *gh* sounding like "p" (/p/), and certainly not at the start of a word (though it can sound like "f" (/f/) at the end of words like "cou**gh**," "lau**gh**," and "enou**gh**"). *Ough* can sound like the long "o" or short "u" vowel sounds, but only when following a consonant. Because a native English speaker would not recognize the *gh* at the start of this word as the consonant "p" sound, they'd be more likely to pronounce the first part of this word simply as "go." From there, they would look for common letter groupings that they recognize as working together to create sounds. They'd see *ph* and assume it was meant to be pronounced as "f." They'd see the letter combination *the* and probably assume the *igh* that follows should be silent. Or they might recognize the arrangement of letters spelling out the English word "height" in the middle and work out the unknown syllables around it. The doubled *tt* could then be pronounced the same as a single *t*, and *eau* is a common word ending that sounds like the long "o."

The location of a word in an English sentence plays an integral role in informing what part of speech it is. Similarly, the location of a phoneme or syllable in an English word plays an integral role in informing how it is pronounced. Every native English speaker has unconsciously accepted this as part of how they rapidly sound out new words and skim across familiar ones. *Eau* is a common letter combination that is derived from French. It only makes the long "o" sound found in "plat**eau**" when it is at the end of a word. A similar rule applies to the *ette* in "gaz**ette**." No native English speaker accidentally reads the word "**beau**tiful" (/ˈbjuːtɪfəl/) as "boetiful" (/ˈboʊːtɪfəl/), for instance, even though it contains the same *eau* letter combination. A native English speaker intuitively recognizes that the placement of a grouping of letters in a word affects its pronunciation. The name "**Beau**" is spelled the same as the first four letters of "**beau**tiful," yet it takes on the "Bo" (/boʊ/) sound, not "Bew" (/bjuː/), because its *eau* letter grouping comes at the end of the word.

Foreign English learners have none of these unconscious pattern-recognizing advantages. They are often taught to look at the English alphabet in the same mechanistic way that works with alphabets with fewer emergent rules and derivations away from a one-to-one correspondence between symbol and sound. Because of this, it is necessary to learn written English through exposure to phonemes, syllables, and words instead of trying to derive how everything *should* be spelled based on a rudimentary understanding of the alphabet. Foreign learners must acquire basic familiarity with potential spelling options before they can make informed guesses at the most likely way to pronounce a syllable or word they read (and how to spell a syllable or word they hear). Every native English speaker does this all the time, just with a much smaller error rate than the foreign learner. Even professional native English narrators and voiceover artists still need to look up the pronunciation of new words when performing their craft. Even professional writers need spell checkers.

Reading from Whole Words

Children learning to read English as their native language start with simple texts containing short and consistently pronounced words (e.g., "The fat cat sat on the mat."). They'll often use picture books like the classic *Goodnight Moon* by Margaret Wise Brown, which features images of objects children already know along with simple descriptions. The juxtaposition creates a lasting mental association between what is pictured and its written label. The names of the objects are also presented in a rhyming manner, such as "bears sitting on chairs" and "kittens with mittens." This gives young learners clues about how to read them. If they can pronounce the first word in the sequence, they will stand a good chance at figuring out how to pronounce the second word (or vice versa), even if it uses different spelling to produce the same syllable.

The same problem applies in the opposite direction when learning to write English. It isn't easy to guess the right spelling for every English word, even if learners can pronounce them correctly. There are too many potentially valid combinations of letters that can produce the sounds of many common words. That's why it is better to approach English with many conclusions (e.g., valid ways of spelling common words) already in mind. The task of effective English teachers is to find ways to seed students' minds with words they can easily recognize in reading and replicate in writing. These common and easy-to-read/spell words form the basis of their contextual understanding of more difficult words. Teaching high-frequency English words provides meaningful context for recognizing whole words and enhances reading speed and comprehension.

Fluent English readers quickly move from word to word as they scan along the written lines of a page. The fastest can chunk many words together and process them instantly as phrasal units, predicting and identifying words in their parafoveal vision based on context before they are even directly focused on.

A similar thing happens to competent English speakers when spontaneously phrasing sentences aloud. They aren't thinking of one word to put in front of another at a time; they are thinking of short phrases or whole sentences. Speakers and writers alike only slow down and process words on the level of their individual components when they encounter ones they don't already know or with highly unconventional spelling or pronunciation. In those cases, even native English speakers might need to sound a word out by letter or syllable and could still be wrong.

There's no reason foreign English learners can't begin to read like native English speakers do as children: with phonetically simple picture books that make meaning and pronunciation easy to grasp as whole words. Adult learners have no reason to be self-conscious about such a juvenile approach. Children's books are designed to be easy to read for people who are new to the madness of English spelling. Unlike young children, however, adult foreign learners will quickly grow past the need for them and be ready to tackle more advanced English reading material.

What can come after simple children's texts for foreign English learners? Like all things about learning English, it depends on what will be most useful and entertaining for each learner. For instance, a tradesperson or someone mechanically inclined can read instructional manuals for their tools, appliances, and devices. Such guides are usually written in concise and straightforward language so they won't be misunderstood. Because it's a subject the learner is already familiar with, they will have a higher chance of understanding objects and actions described with unfamiliar words. Once they've learned the most important words by rote (e.g., "insert," "screw," "hammer," "nail," "place," "secure," "add," "front," "back," "turn," etc.), the missing pieces are much easier to fill in. Their working map of practical English understanding will quickly grow.

If someone goes out to eat at cafes or restaurants often, the menus offered in such establishments might be the perfect introduction to practical, real-world English reading for them. Like with instructional manuals, the vocabulary and phrasing will usually be limited to a food-and-dining-appropriate context. The reader will know that whatever words they can't immediately read will somehow concern what goes into a dish or how it is served. The most common ingredients or names of popular drinks or meals will be easy to learn for someone who regularly orders and consumes them. Someone who eats a lot of steak and drinks a lot of martinis should know the names of these things in English. From there, they might soon learn how to describe how a steak is cooked and a martini mixed. The most basic level of understanding quickly becomes more nuanced, but only if the learners are engaged in what they are learning.

Let's not overlook some of the simplest and most prolific written English communication: advertisements. Whether or not you have any inherent interest in the products or services being marketed, the sheer repetition of them in a place where

English speakers reside should aid considerably in learning their key terminology. Billboards, business cards, commercials, internet pop-up and banner ads, and more offer the opportunity to read and hear simple slogans and product pitches. Learners just need to be aware that abbreviated forms of communication often default to slang and sentence fragments that don't represent proper English.

These and any other type of simple English texts can be found in the wild anywhere English is used. Manufacturers will usually include English and other common world languages in all their instruction manuals and on their product packaging to maximize the chances of customers being able to read them. But even in the worst cases where access to real-world English text in one's native environment is rare, English versions of all these common materials can easily be searched for online and compared to local language versions.

The Motivation to Read and Write

I once worked with an illiterate teenager in a rural non-English-speaking indigenous community. He never learned to read or write any language at all, though he could speak his native language as well as his family and neighbors could. His parents and local community never demonstrated to him (or maybe never even understood themselves) that it would be a valuable asset for their son to understand and use written language. What resources and inspiration would he need at such a relatively late stage in life to finally learn to read?

Foremost, he would need the desire to learn. Nothing that I or anyone else could do for him would matter without that. And why should he want to learn to read? He's lived his entire life so far not being able to. Why should he exert the effort to adopt an ability he's never needed before? Thus far, he has lived his life in such a way that he has managed to get what he needs without communicating his thoughts in written language or reading the written thoughts of others. There have always been people around him who can read and write on his behalf. But his illiteracy is still a handicap. It's equivalent to needing an interpreter for everything he does. He relies on constant access to people who can read and write to derive the value of written text. All people who can read and write understand at least some of its value, even if many fail to employ it fully.

How can anyone make a teenager who has never been interested in learning to read and write suddenly become curious enough to start pursuing it? They can demonstrate its utility in ways that matter on a personal level. They can show him how many useful and interesting things he can do if he can read and write. These motivations are different for each learner and change with each stage of their development. The teacher's job is to figure out what they are and adapt their teaching to match them.

My unconventional approach with this illiterate young man was something not directly related to reading or English: I gave him a handful of guitar classes.

At first, he couldn't even recognize the seven letters of the Latin alphabet used in the Western note-naming system (*a* through *g*). He soon had to learn to associate these strange symbols with shapes his fingers would make when pressed into chords against the guitar fretboard. I also found that with the smallest amount of instruction in his native language, he could see the relationship between the lines and dots used for guitar chord diagrams and how his fingers should be arranged. Though they lack a traditional alphabet, these diagrams still constitute forms of reading because the guitar player must derive information to integrate and actions to take from written symbols.

A

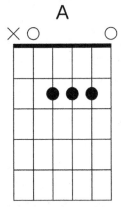

"A Major Chord" by Kitsuney is licensed under Creative Commons Attribution-ShareAlike 4.0 International. https://creativecommons.org/licenses/by-sa/4.0/

"A Major Guitar Chord" by Mjchael is licensed under Creative Commons Attribution-ShareAlike 4.0 International. https://creativecommons.org/licenses/by-sa/4.0/

As soon as this young man realized that he could make the instrument sound a certain way by following simple pictographic instructions, he became incentivized to learn to read more of them. Each new recognizable symbol directly correlated with greater ability in a skill he now valued (i.e., the ability to make music from the guitar). For the first time in his life, he had a personal reason to study how to read written symbols because he saw an immediate benefit. This self-imposed study soon led him to recognize and play every basic chord on the guitar (e.g., C major, E minor, A7, and so forth) with greater proficiency than many of the Western, literate, and educated adults I'd taught before. My student only had to be shown that this form of reading would enable him to do something he was organically motivated toward. I used the opportunity of the excitement he felt from reading these basic labels to also teach him the letters used in his name and the names of his family members. Once the ball was in motion, extending his enthusiasm to other reading applications he otherwise might not have been interested in was easy.

Now here's an interesting thought experiment: If the illiterate teenage boy I knew would bother to undertake the effort required to learn to read and write fluently, which language might prove most useful to him throughout his life? Is it possible that English could end up providing greater value for him in the long run than his local language, which is only used by the people living in his small country? Learning to read is a huge cognitive investment. If he puts his time and energy into it, learning to read English might offer a better return on that investment than learning to read his local language (or any others). On an absolute scale, reading and writing in English can offer far more opportunities.

It's also worth considering the *relative* value of acquiring a skill that few other people nearby have. Because everyone around him already reads and writes in his local language, he has been able to function so far without being able to. The skill is prevalent enough that others can perform it for him as needed. But few of those same people can read and write in English. That makes English literacy comparatively valuable because of how locally scarce it is. If something needs to be read or written in English, he will be one of the only people in his area who can do it. It's easy to imagine him being in a position where everyone in his village comes to him when they need an instruction manual from an English-language product translated for them, for instance.

CHAPTER 7

ENGLISH GRAMMAR

IN CONVENTIONAL EFL education, learning simple vocabulary is prioritized over learning grammar. The philosophy behind this approach seems to be that the more words the learner recognizes and can translate back into their native language, the better they must be at English. They get more "English points" for demonstrating familiarity with a larger amount of words. There is only enough administrative bandwidth to evaluate effectiveness by directly measurable metrics like "number of words memorized," which is an easy category to quantify and grade via standardized methodology. Focusing on vocabulary like this is logistically backward and not the most viable way to attain conversational fluency compared to meaningful contextualized learning.[74]

After establishing the basics of pronunciation and reading, it becomes far easier to start instilling the principles of English's structure. Basic oral and literacy skills create a foundation for understanding and applying grammar rules. New applications of those principles can later follow via a gradually increasing repertoire of words and phrases that learners can transform and iterate upon at will.

Without a structural understanding of most of English's rules, memorizing more words is like accumulating more

---

[74] Nation, P. (2001). Learning vocabulary in another language. Cambridge University Press.

physical possessions without a place to store and organize them. Buying a dozen new specialized kitchen appliances won't make you more adept in the kitchen if you don't know where to put them and how to use them. They'll just become clutter and get in your way, reducing your effectiveness. You need shelves, drawers, cabinets, hooks, and boxes to organize them and enable their unused potential and prevent them from becoming counterproductive obstacles.

Learners, of course, need enough words to get started communicating or understanding anything in English. They must recognize enough high-frequency incidentals to start picking up on grammar, pronunciation, and spelling principles. For most people, grammar nerds notwithstanding, attempting to learn grammar in isolation ends up feeling quite dull. Most learners will want to be able to do something interesting or useful with English soon enough. Learners always need some amount of short-term reward and gratification. However, those instant results do not have to come at the expense of the fundamentals of grammar.

Proper grammar is also not the be-all and end-all of English communication. You can say many grammatically correct things that technically make sense in English but still come across as dull, awkward, odd, or difficult to understand. Style matters too. If you make a clunky, vague, or redundant run-on sentence, you're not clearly communicating an idea, no matter how perfectly you conjugate it. This is often the case when foreigners try to use terms and constructions that they haven't fully acclimated to.[75]

---

[75] A similar problem can happen with native English writers who feel obligated to shoehorn five-dollar words in when fifty-cent words would do. They don't normally phrase things the way they force themselves to when writing, so it comes across as awkward and unnatural. There's a clear difference with writers who just naturally think and express them-

Grammar describes the principles of changing and combining words to create emergent meaning. A word is the product of the emergent meaning between syllables. Combining words in a certain order creates an idea that does not exist in any of those words individually. To do that effectively, we need to understand the English parts of speech, such as the difference between an adjective, a verb, a noun, an article, and a preposition. We need to understand the syntax of how the order of words changes their relationship to each other and, therefore, the new meaning they create together by coexisting in the same sentence.

Information can be anything, like a word, but an idea is a complete sentence with cohesive meaning. Anything ungrammatical becomes nonsense. Even seemingly ungrammatical slang is only decipherable through the improvised formation of new grammatical rules,[76] implied grammar in omitted words,[77] or obviously intended grammar when the wrong words are used.[78] It's not due to the limits of English that language learners cannot get away with expressing ungrammatical ideas but because of the inherent logical limits

selves in complex or even what may be considered pretentious ways; it's their authentic voice coming across on the page.

[76] Such as with the slang contraction "ain't" for "am not" or "are not" or the use of "be" instead of "is" or "are" to indicate regular action, known as "habitual be" in African American Vernacular English (AAVE), a.k.a. Ebonics.

[77] Such as when a sentence fragment refers to an already established grammatical construction. If someone asks, "How are you?," answering with just the word "fine" is enough to imply a full grammatical construction: "I am fine."

[78] "There are less apples on the tree" contains incorrect grammar, but is still something many native English speakers would say and understand. The correct construction would use "fewer apples" because "apples" is a countable noun. However, the incorrect word "less" still serves the understandable and intended grammatical function of denoting a smaller amount.

of the mind and how it deals with concepts.[79] Sentences that ignore the meaning of words and logical grammar rules are just random word orderings. Every complete idea, every real sentence, has emergent meaning. There's a difference between the thought of a giraffe (or even the word "giraffe") and the complete, coherent idea that "giraffes are tall," "I like giraffes," or "giraffes eat leaves."

Identifying Parts of Speech and Sentence Structure

Imagine that the only words you can use in English are **nouns**. What will the limits of your communication be? You will probably sound like Tarzan or a caveman. All descriptive qualities, all actions, and all relationships between nouns will have to be implied by things like physical gesturing or contextual clues. You won't even be able to use the most basic verbs like "is/are" to denote identification between nouns.

"Me: Tarzan. You: Jane. This: Table. That: Food."

What's implied by these fragments (and what would be stated in proper English) is:

"I *am* Tarzan. You *are* Jane. This *is a* table. That *is* food."

If all I say is, "this: food," the implication is that the thing I am referring to belongs to the category of concepts called food. It also implies that you (the listener) know the purpose of food. You know you're supposed to eat it. Otherwise, why would I be identifying for you that the thing in front of me is food? I'm implying you can eat this if you want to. But I cannot give you instructions for what actions you can or should

---

[79] Noam Chomsky's theory of Universal Grammar (UG) proposes the existence of an innate grammar that is hardwired in the human brain with principles and rules common to all languages.

take with the food under these conditions of such limited communication. I cannot form complex thoughts and communicate nuance and detail to others because I cannot even describe the actions you should be taking or how you should be taking them.

Without **adjectives**, you can't modify your nouns to make them more descriptive, like "hot food" or "rotten food," even though such details might be crucial to your intended meaning. Without **prepositions**, you cannot show the relationships between things, such as eating a "plate *of* food." Eating *with* a fork is quite a different action than eating a fork. Lacking the ability to conjugate **verbs** into past or future tenses, everything you say is interpreted as being immediately or generally occurring. You're stuck with a very primitive, direct, and present way of signifying what you want. **Conjunctions** grant the ability to link concepts together as part of the same category or as alternatives. How do you indicate you are referring to more than one thing at a time, whether concrete or conceptual, unless you can use vital connecting words like "and" and "or"? Even **articles**, like the words "the" and "a/an," reveal the level of specificity you intend when you communicate a thought. Are you talking about that one specific thing? Or any one of a possible group containing things of that description? "I like **the** big dog" (specific), "I like **a** big dog" (non-specific), or "I like big **dogs**" (general and plural) mean different things.

When an intermediate student of English encounters a sentence they can't fully understand, an invisible process goes on in their mind to decipher it. The more they can see the grammatical structure linking the words they know, the easier it is to infer the meaning of the ones they don't. Native English speakers do the same thing, of course. We are all quickly inferring the meaning of words we don't perfectly know by filling in their place in the sentence based on what we do understand. When you hear or read an English sentence, how long does it take you to determine its subject? Do you ever get confused about which words are nouns, verbs, adjectives, or something else? If the sentence contains a word you don't know, can you still infer what relationship that word has with every other word?

Some English parts of speech are easily identified because of certain letter combinations or suffixes that are frequently applied to them. Adjectives often end in *–y*, *–ic*, *–ish*, *–ive*, *–ient*, *–able*, *–al*, *–ful*, or *–ous*. Adverbs often end in *–ly*, *–ally*, or *–ily*. These patterns are consistent enough that English speakers can improvise turning nouns into adjectives and adverbs by simply adding these suffixes, fully expecting to be understood by other English speakers. We verb**ify** nouns with *–en*, *–ate*, *–ify*, or *–ize*. To move in the opposite direction would be to noun**ify** verbs or adjectives. Suffixes such as *–ication*, *–ification*, *–ization*, and *–ation* help us denote when this change in part of speech has occurred and a previously non-noun word has undergone noun**ification**.[80] Other noun suffixes like *–er*, *–ist*, *–tion*, *–ity*, *–ance*, *–hood*, *–dom*, *–ment*, and *–ness* clearly stand out as belonging to things instead of actions. Verbs are likewise easy to identify if they have been conjugated with an obvious verb suffix (such as *–ed*[81] or *–ing*[82]) or that have

---

[80] In this instance, I've committed two separate acts of part-of-speech transformation. I first implied the existence of a verb, "to nounify" (derived from the noun "noun"), and then changed that verb back into a different noun meaning the process of that verb, "nounification."

[81] Except in cases where the conjugated verbal plays the part of a past participle, which functions as an adjective (e.g., Ag**ed** cheese tastes so much better.")

[82] Except in cases where the conjugated verbal plays the part of a gerund, which functions as a noun (e.g., "Eat**ing** is my favorite pastime."), or a

auxiliary words in front clearly indicating conjugation (such as "will" or "have," or "to" in the unconjugated state).

All these features serve as grammatical clues about what is happening in an English sentence at a glance, even if you don't know the meaning of every word. They form a map that is essential to understanding sentences not already encountered and memorized by rote. There is no way for the foreign English learner to begin adapting to the endless possible computations of English words that form coherent sentences unless they have been taught to recognize grammatical structure when they encounter it.

Suppose an intermediate English learner encounters this sentence for the first time:

"In many cultures around the world, the husband is expected to be dominant, but the wife is expected to be obedient."

If they know every word in that sentence except the last one, "obedient," they should be able to figure out what it means from contextual clues. They should recognize that being "obedient" is somehow contrasted with being "dominant" (which means containing the quality of dominating). Perhaps the learner already knows the verb "to obey" and has seen the common ending *–ient* used with English adjectives. They can connect those ideas in their mind and understand that an obedient person is probably someone who obeys a lot. They can't make that contextual connection if they can't recognize the grammar of what's being said and infer what they are missing.

---

present participle, which functions as an adjective (e.g., "Crying children are so annoying.").

This elaborate recognition process becomes automatic as the learner approaches conversational fluency. A native speaker does not have to consciously remember that countable nouns need to be accompanied by indefinite articles and uncountable nouns do not. The two categories just seem different to them. They know they can hold "**a** book" and conceptualize it as something with its own definable boundaries. They cannot do the same with "**an** air" or "**a** furniture." They intuitively understand that these concepts make more sense if we pair them with a countable unit of measurement, such as "a **roomful of** air" or "a **piece of** furniture."

The Ordering of Syntax

In addition to affixes that denote grammatical function and relationships between words, English relies on syntax (i.e., word order), which is fairly concise and consistent compared to many languages. English speakers are spared the trouble of memorizing endless individual changes to every noun and verb that they encounter. Adjectives always precede the nouns they are modifying. Subject nouns always precede the verbs they are acting out. Object nouns always come after the verbs that denote action being done to them.

English morphology is limited. With nouns, you can add –s or –es to change from singular to plural (except with irregular plurals like "geese" and "children"). You can add an apostrophe (–'s or –s') to indicate possessiveness (singular and plural, respectively). There's nothing you need to change about a noun to indicate its gender (which doesn't exist in English except in the third-person singular pronouns "he" and "she" and their derivatives[83]). There's also nothing

---

[83] Such as their corresponding object pronouns ("him" and "her"), posses-

to change about a noun to indicate its relationship to other nouns. That role is filled by prepositions like "of," "from," and "to."

In languages with looser rules of syntax, learners cannot necessarily rely on the order of the information to determine the structure and parse the relationships between words. They must pay attention to other subtle clues, such as how verbs are conjugated to indicate subject and object relationships or special prefixes, infixes, and suffixes added to words. More explicit units of information must be taken in and deciphered to avoid the possibility of more than one potentially valid interpretation of the same word arrangement. They might have to listen to the entire sentence before they can piece together how all the parts go together. Clear and consistent word ordering in English sentences simplifies the process of recognizing structure.

In English, "the cat bites the dog" means the direct inverse of "the dog bites the cat." The subject and object are inverted by reversing the order of nouns. The common subject-verb-object (SVO) ordering of English is so fundamental that we accept it as obvious once we are used to it. In most cases, it intuitively makes sense to put the most important information (such as the subject and the action it is taking) at the beginning of the sentence and get less important as the sentence goes on. If the speaker gets cut off before finishing the sentence or the reader only glances at the first half, the most important information will still be communicated. Especially for longer sentences with lots of modifiers and clauses, putting the most important information upfront makes it easier to keep it in mind as the rest of the sentence unfolds.

---

sive pronouns ("his," "her," and "hers"), and reflexive pronouns ("himself" and "herself").

The whole structure, with its full emergent meaning, comes into focus with the lowest cognitive strain:

"The tall boy walks to school through the baseball field every Tuesday at nine a.m. with his friend Susy."

In this sentence, the most important information comes first. "The tall boy" is the subject. What does the tall boy do? He walks. Where does he walk? To school. How does he get there? Through the baseball field. When and how often? Every Tuesday at nine a.m. With whom? His friend. Which friend? Susy. Each new piece of information elaborates logically and clearly upon the preceding information. We must first know that this sentence is about a tall boy walking to school. That's already a complete idea on its own.[84] Everything else depends on that. In most cases, starting with any other information in this sentence, such as the day and time he does something, how he gets somewhere, and whom he does something with, won't make as much sense.

"The tall boy walks *to school*" is already much more revealing. Now, not only do we now know which boy this is and where he is going, but we also have an implied purpose for his visit. Lacking any other clarifying information, our natural tendency is to assume he is going there to attend class and learn something, especially since 9 a.m. is a common time for classes to start. The speaker communicating this information almost certainly knows this and chooses what to include or omit based on this assumed shared understanding.[85]

---

[84] We could break this sentence down even further to its shortest grammatical construction containing just the subject and predicate in their most bare form: "The boy walks." However, both the noun "boy" and the verb "to walk" are so generic that they fail to paint a vivid picture. Without further context, it's likely the listener is going to want more information about the boy and his walking.

[85] They would likely specify the purpose if it were something other than

English breaks this basic convention of starting with the independent clause containing the most important information when the speaker considers some other information to be a higher priority or for stylistic flow:

> **"Through the baseball field every Tuesday at 9 a.m.**, the tall boy walks to school with his friend Susy."

> **"With his friend Susy**, the tall boy walks to school through the baseball field every Tuesday at 9 a.m."

In these cases, we bring phrases that should normally be somewhere in the back of the sentence to the front to call attention to them. This necessitates setting them apart by a comma in writing (and usually a small pause in speaking). Maybe it really matters that the listener first understands how the boy gets to school, at what day and time, or with which friend he is going there. The fact that these re-ordered sentences begin with prepositions ("through" and "with," respectively) is a clue for learners as to the structure of the sentence they are about to receive.

The Temporality of Tenses

English features clear and consistent grammatical tenses for conjugating verbs. This fact goes a long way toward reducing the unnecessary cognitive load of thinking in the language and spontaneously restructuring ideas to improve clarity regarding time. Other languages might have six distinct endings for every verb that depend on the subject performing the

---

we naturally expect it to be when a boy visits a school. Maybe he's going there to feed a stray cat he's seen there before. Maybe his band meets there to practice on weekends.

verb and its plurality: first-person singular and plural ("I" and "we"), second-person singular and plural ("you" and "you all"), and third-person singular and plural ("he/she/it" and "they"). Infinitive verbs can also belong to different categories of letter endings, each carrying unique sets of six distinct conjugated endings for each tense. Many languages will often omit the subject and have it implied by how the verb is conjugated, requiring inference from the listener or reader to determine which noun is taking which action with which adjectival qualities, while English speakers conventionally rely on explicitly stating the subject as a noun or pronoun to denote who is doing what.

English can't rely on the way a verb is conjugated to denote subjects because it has only a few verb endings to remember (so long as we disregard irregulars). Adding –s or –es applies exclusively to the third-person singular in the present simple tense. The rest of the present simple doesn't require changing a verb's ending from its infinitive form. We add –ing to indicate continuous tenses where things are, were, or will be actively happening. And for the past, all verbs take on the –d or –ed ending. All other tense changes are indicated by adding auxiliary words before the verb, i.e., conjugations of "have" and "be."

Much information about a verb's relationship with time is revealed by which of the four types (simple, continuous, perfect, and perfect continuous)[86] of three temporal perspectives (past, present, and future) we use. Correctly employing these 12 possible tenses imbues dynamic temporal meaning

---

[86] In English, the continuous tenses can also interchangeably be called "progressive," though there is technically a subtle distinction between them. Continuous is what you do in an ongoing manner (e.g., "I am **studying** to become a doctor."), and progressive is what you are doing immediately (e.g., "I am **eating** lunch right now.").

to sentences. Native speakers of languages that lack these distinctions frequently underestimate them and incorrectly interchange them when learning English. For example, they might not appreciate the difference between something that happens *generally* (present simple) and something that is happening *actively* (present continuous). Saying "I play golf *right now*," which would be the most direct translation from a language lacking continuous tenses, sounds awkward to native English speakers who would default to "I am *playing* golf."

The perfect tenses in English tend to be even harder for foreign learners to grok, particularly the difference between the *past simple* and *present perfect* tense. It is the difference between something that *happened* and something that *has happened*. The past simple tense generally denotes an event that happened and ceased to happen sometime in the past. The specific time of its occurrence and/or ceasing may be indicated, or it may not. But the implication is that the thing's happening is contained to an incidental occurrence in the past.

Even though it is one of the four *present* tenses, the present perfect tense also references the *past*. The difference is that it references the past *leading up to* the present. Indeed, all perfect tenses cover a range of time up to the perspective indicated. The past perfect refers to the past leading up to a point further ahead in the past (the past of the past). The present perfect refers to the past leading up to the present (the past of the present). Most confusingly, the future perfect refers to a past that has not yet happened, leading up to a point further ahead in the future (the past of the future). Making any of these perfect tenses continuous with *–ing* adds the quality of them actively happening during their denoted periods.

Copious use of perfect tenses might start to feel like time travel for a foreign English learner who is not accustomed to them. But their communication possibilities make English grammatically convenient for denoting temporal relationships between things and actions. This aspect of English grammar is frequently neglected in EFL. Learners who can use all simple and continuous tenses flawlessly might avoid employing a perfect tense where it would be more appropriate and might miss the precise temporal meaning indicated by someone else using one.

Using the perfect tenses can be further complicated because we indicate them by adding the auxiliary verb "have" before the main verb, and we also use "to have" as a main verb. Have you ever heard a student say "had not" or "hadn't" when they should have said "did not have" or "didn't have"?[87]

What if you conjugate the main verb "to have" in one of the perfect tenses? That's how you can end up with the seemingly excessive repetition of the same word in grammatically valid ways.

> Present simple: "I **have** the flu." This is the normal way to conjugate and use the verb "to have."
>
> Present perfect: "I **have had** the flu already."
>
> Past perfect: "I **had had** the flu before."
>
> Future perfect: "I **will have had** the flu by then."

---

[87] The student in this case confused auxiliary "have" for main "have." "She **hadn't** a book" is not the negative form of "she **had** a book." We must add the auxiliary verb "do" to form the negative for "have." "She **didn't have** a book" is correct.

These are all normal and understandable ways to have two "haves" in sequence. The first "have," "had," or "will have" is the auxiliary verb indicating a perfect tense. The second "have" or "had" is the main verb indicating the action of possessing or obtaining something. But the repetition doesn't stop there. We can easily fit three or four "haves" together. Consider this triple-have sentence:

"The flu that I **have had has** been very bad."

Here, we find a first-person present auxiliary "have," a first-person past main "had," and a third-person present auxiliary "has." This construction is valid because there are functionally two subjects in the sentence: "The flu" and "I." The phrase "that I have had" functions as an adjectival modifier for "the flu." We can then stretch this to four sequential "haves" by making both subjects have something as conjugated in perfect tenses.

"The flu that I **have had has had** a big effect on me."

And if we conjugate "to have" in the past perfect tense twice, we will end up with the word "had" four times in a row:

"The flu that I **had had had had** a big effect on me."[88]

---

[88] Similar word repetitions can be achieved with the auxiliary verbs "do" (e.g., "The homework that I **did do does** not count.") and "will" (e.g., "Soon, I **will will** my way up the corporate ladder.") since they are also main verbs.

CHAPTER 8

ENGLISH VOCABULARY

ALTHOUGH IT IS given the most credence in conventional EFL, vocabulary is the least important aspect of English acquisition. Memorizing new words has the smallest bearing on one's ability to communicate effectively in English. It is also easier to add new words to a working vocabulary *after* the organizational principles that apply to those words and the forms they can take (i.e., grammar) have been integrated. Yet, a conventional EFL teacher typically assigns their students lists of words and phrases to take home, drill, and memorize before the next class. When it comes, the students might have barely bothered looking at the words they are mandated to learn. Why has this happened? The teacher has given their students vocabulary they had no natural motivation to learn. The task of effective EFL teachers is to figure out how to make learning English as intrinsically rewarding as possible: to make the act of learning itself rewarding.

Learning vocabulary requires personal prioritization. How does the learner decide which, out of the tens of thousands of English words they are likely to come across, are the most important to focus on first? The answer is obvious because the same principle guides the entire language acquisition process: whatever is most useful or interesting to learn. They should focus on learning the words that will directly increase their ability to communicate in ways that matter to them. As well, we have to consider that learners are much more likely to recall new terms and adopt them into unconscious memory if they encounter and actively put them into practice, which will only happen if they are words the learner has reason to use in their English communication. The old advice about it being easier to remember someone new's name if you use it in conversation immediately after learning it applies all the same to new English terms. Learners need to start recognizing and using them right away, and they're not going to do that just because their teacher commanded them to under threat of extrinsic punishment.

If an EFL learner goes out to eat at restaurants and cafes often, they will do well to learn the vocabulary associated with ordering items off the menu. If they enjoy reading science fiction stories, they should learn the type of words they are likely to encounter, such as terminology related to technology and space travel. If they enjoy playing sports with their friends, they should learn words related to passing, shooting, scoring, and teamwork. And if some learners happen to be supreme language nerds obsessed with digesting every new word imaginable, they might as well just read a dictionary for fun. They won't have the same practicality or prioritization problems as everyone else. They will consume new words as they encounter them and seek out as many interesting terms as their minds can hold.

Imperfect Synonyms and Nuance

Any time you replace one word with another, you somehow change the meaning of your communication. Whether the change is good or bad depends on how you intend what you communicate to be received. Everyone selects the best term they know out of all that come to mind in their internal lexicon. The spontaneous selection process gets faster and easier the more words someone knows and the more experience they have conveying the nuances captured by each option. It happens so quickly that most native English speakers are hardly conscious of doing it, except during the occasional brain fart that interrupts the automatic process.

The lexical selection process is more difficult for foreign English learners. Under conventional conditions, they usually learn new words as equivalents to words from their native languages. And so, they miss out on all the subtle differences between how the word might be used in English compared to the native equivalent. They might also overlook all the other English synonyms with subtly differing connotations. They will often simply be presented with a list of English synonyms and told that all these words can and should be used interchangeably. The more variety in synonyms foreign English speakers stuff into their sentences, the better at English they seem to think they will be perceived to be.

Indeed, much of what makes a foreigner sound like a foreigner (beyond an obvious foreign accent) is the use of words and phrases with unintended associations. Due to conventional EFL's emphasis on rote vocabulary memorization, learners will often opt to use difficult words when simple ones would be better for the context they are speaking in. Ironically, the attempts at making international students appear adept at English actually make them worse at using the language for communication.

Foreign learners might not be able to easily infer the superiority or inferiority of choosing a word like "courageous" over a mostly synonymous one like "brave" in a specific context. But native speakers will know which one intuitively feels better to them, even if they cannot explain the subtle differences between these two. They will only experience a mild sense of inappropriateness when one is used where the other should have been. So long as I have been taught that words like "courageous" and "brave" are interchangeable English synonyms, I won't be able to use each of them as appropriately as possible. They mean similar things. They can be used with a similar kind of effect in many situations. But there are times when a competent native English speaker would opt to say "courageous" instead of "brave" and vice-versa.

"Courageous" is more formal than "brave." It's a more active and powerful term. Bravery is a more passive quality than courageousness. If you call Superman brave, it doesn't do the character justice. Yes, he's certainly brave, like all heroes, but he's also much more than that. He's *Superman*, the epitome of heroism. He's not just a brave guy. Bravery feels more casual to a native English speaker. It's an inactive attribute. Courage consists of intentional and premeditated acts of bravery. Bravery could describe any spontaneous reaction to risk, but courage is willful and deliberate. It's a brave person who would jump in front of a gun to save someone's life. Meanwhile, soldiers choosing to go off to fight for something they believe in is courageous because their actions require conscious thought and planning. Courage is a subset of bravery, a specific way of being brave.

A common thesaurus might tell you that a brave person can also be called adventurous, audacious, confident, daring, dashing, fearless, foolhardy, gallant, gutsy, heroic, reckless, resolute, spirited, spunky, stout, strong, or valiant. All these words are related, but some mean quite different things that you would not want to mix up in your communication. Native English speakers generally learn the connotations of such near-synonyms by hearing and using them regularly, coming to associate slightly different feelings with each. They start to feel differently about what they're trying to express. That's why a native English speaker likely wouldn't confuse "foolhardy" or "reckless" for "brave." "Foolhardy" means prone to doing something foolish, something that is likely going to fail. "Reckless" means disregarding risk. "Brave," on the contrary, means having the emotional capacity to face and overcome risk. A brave or courageous person must know the risk involved in their actions. Recklessness implies that you don't think about the danger: You're unaware of what the danger is, or you don't care.

"Gutsy" is another subset of "brave." Colloquially, it means someone who has a lot of guts. They're willing to do things other people aren't. However, it's still not exactly the same as being brave. It has a more rough and informal feeling to it. Firefighters who rush into burning buildings to save lives are not being gutsy. Someone who performs dangerous stunts on a motorcycle might be, though. An average-looking dude approaching a supermodel to ask her on a date is definitely gutsy.

Consider the subtle connotative differences between other near-synonyms like "enormous," "imposing," and "towering" when describing a large dog. Does the writer/speaker merely mean to convey that the dog is bigger than average in size? If so, is there any reason to use superfluous adjectives like "enormous," "imposing," or "towering"? These near-synonyms are all subsets of the umbrella concept of "big," but saying "the big dog" versus "the enormous, imposing, and/or towering dog" communicates a different idea. The writer/speaker must determine if it's important to know such details.

"Towering," to a native English speaker, implies something about how you feel in the presence of a very tall person. When I use the word "towering," I imagine a man so tall that he's practically covering me when I stand next to him. It indicates something about the subjective experience of being near this tall person, which is different from a flat objective description of tallness (meaning greater-than-average height). When a non-native English speaker wants to talk about something tall and uses the word "towering" as an arbitrary substitute for it, it becomes clear that there is something wrong with this person's understanding of English.

How many common near-synonyms could you articulate the difference between to a non-native English speaker?

- happen, befall, and occur[89]
- need, require, and demand[90]
- kill, execute, and murder[91]
- save, aid, and rescue[92]

---

[89] Befalling is a type of happening that indicates active unavoidability and serious consequences, as though some natural force has imposed what has happened. The common choice of prepositions paired with each hints toward this. Anything can "happen *to*" you. Something serious requiring active attention "befalls *upon*" you. Occurring is a more detached and formal way to describe something that happens.

[90] "Need" describes lacking something that would lead to a defined outcome. "Require" is more firm and formal, as if to indicate that the requirement is not just one effective way to achieve the outcome but that it absolutely cannot be achieved without it. "Demand" is an active need calling attention to itself, created by important circumstances lacking something.

[91] To kill something is to end its life. Execution is the formalized process of killing for officially sanctioned reasons. Murder is the intentional and unwarranted killing of an innocent human being.

[92] Saving is the base category for protecting from harm and preventing a negative outcome. "Aid" means to provide assistance and support. Rescuing is a more proactive and premeditated type of saving that usually implies immediately intervening to remove someone from a threatening situation or removing an active threat.

- friend, buddy, and comrade[93]

What about "small" and "little"? Does the difference seem inconsequential? Would recommending a book called *The Small Prince* or *Small Women* or a movie called *The Small Mermaid* feel intuitively wrong to you? Is it just because you have familiarity with those titles as *The Little Prince, Little Women,* and *The Little Mermaid*? Or do you carry different associations for things that are small and things that are little?[94] Can you transfer these associations to foreign English learners so that they start to use these near-synonyms as appropriately as you do?

Formal, Informal, Colloquial, and Slang Terminology

Formal language is precise, which makes it more difficult to construct spontaneously. It requires more preparation before delivery. It's why we expect a professionally published book or elegant speech to be expressed better than something written or said off the cuff. Accordingly, the recipients of formal communication are more sensitive to error. These readers and listeners have higher standards because the tone and context have set their expectations.

Informal language is expected to be less precise. It is easier to construct because it requires less planning and fore-

---

[93] "Friend" is the base category for someone with whom you share a positive, mildly intimate social association. "Buddy" is a particular type of friend, typically characterized by casual fun, humor, and shared pastimes. "Comrade" implies positive association through a shared ideology or cause, the most notable of which that frequented this term was the Communist Party of the Soviet Union.

[94] "Small" just captures the general quality of not being very big. "Little" also carries connotations of cuteness, preciousness, and vulnerability, which are important aspects of how we think about the titular prince, women, and mermaid in their respective stories.

thought. It happens more in the moment and asks less of the reader or listener to receive the intended meaning. Often, only the general idea matters, and the consequences for misinterpretation are mild. In recent years, writing has gained the luxury of lesser formality because of technologies that have made it easier for us to communicate in electronic written mediums.[95] Before smartphones and computers, writing was more laborious than speaking, which lent an automatic degree of formality to written words. This is not the case anymore because of how easy it is to communicate spontaneously in writing.[96]

Slang can be thought of as novelty semantics yet to demonstrate durable worth in the lexicon. It's usually innovated by the younger generations experimenting with new ways to express themselves.[97] Slang can be incomprehensible to older people who don't participate in the social circles within which it emerges. But that doesn't make it "wrong" or "fake" English or not still subject to fundamental grammatical patterns.

---

[95] Language teachers often instruct their students that there are different semantic and grammatical rules applied to writing than to speaking, really just meaning that writing is more formal. Ironically, young students attending these classes message their friends in an extremely casual writing style through shortened words and sentence fragments. Foreign English learners will often master the dynamics of informal textspeak better than they learn "real" English because they are more actively immersed in its organic use in their social lives.

[96] In fact, the trend has reversed to a large degree. Many people opt to send short text messages and emails and avoid making phone calls or leaving voice messages. The exception is handwritten letters, which still carry the weight of investment and intention because of how much longer they take to produce than the same words typed out via a keyboard.

[97] Established swear words are not slang, however. They have historical roles in human expression. We use swear words to invoke a tone and emphasis that is not otherwise available. Telling someone to go to hell (or worse) carries greater weight than telling them to get out of here, leave you alone, have a bad day, and so on.

One additional problem with trying to improve vocabulary by formal study is that the colloquial ways we label or describe things are often arbitrary and impossible to infer ahead of exposure. When I was teaching the English vocabulary related to driving a car, one of my students already knew most of the operative terms, such as "gas," "brake," "clutch," "steering wheel," "headlights," and so forth. But she got confused when I kept using the phrase, "step on the accelerator." I had to explain that "accelerator" was another word used for the gas pedal. It makes the car *accelerate* (i.e., speed up) by giving the engine more gas. She asked, "So if we call the gas pedal 'the accelerator' because it makes the car speed up, then we should also call the brake pedal 'the decelerator' because it makes the car slow down, right?"

I didn't know how to explain that no one calls the brake "the decelerator." I didn't know why. I just knew it would sound strange to me and every other American. Technically, the label makes perfect sense. Deceleration is the opposite of acceleration. The brake does the opposite of the gas. Both words are apt descriptions of the function of each pedal. Yet, for reasons that probably no single person knows, Americans have accepted one term and not the other for the pedals in their cars. And there is no way for a foreign English learner to directly infer this information from the meanings of the words. The choice to use one label and not the other is just an arbitrary cultural artifact that one must be exposed to in order to appropriate.[98]

A robot learning English would face no such cultural conundrums in its communication. It would choose the most

---

[98] Furthermore, to a physicist, slowing down is just a form of negative acceleration. You can imagine the confusion that would emerge from referring to the pedals of the car as positive and negative accelerators.

literal and direct term to indicate its intended meaning. It would have to be programmed to account for arbitrary cultural nuances to appear more human. A terminator[99] may respond positively to a statement or request with the word "affirmative" because it is the most direct way to affirm what someone said. No native English-speaking human naturally does this in casual conversation. They say "yes," "ok," "yeah," "uh-huh," "mhmm," "I see," "got it," "understood," "sweet," "sure," "why not?" "I agree," "go for it," "no problemo," "if you say so," "you got it, dude," and so on.

Linguistic reappropriation occurs when a term associated with a fictional concept starts to be used colloquially for related real-world concepts.[100] For example, a local teaching partner planning a lesson with me once asked our group class to talk about their "superpowers and kryptonite." The learners understood the first term because a superpower is something generally associated with superheroes and applied figuratively in real-world contexts to mean anything someone is exceptionally good at. But the second term, "kryptonite," eluded every student in our class. The lesson planner was a fluent non-native English speaker who had

---

[99] Even this reference depends upon an assumed level of pop culture and colloquial English familiarity regarding the word "terminator." Out of context, a terminator is something that terminates. It brings an end to something (such as in the case with genetic transcription terminators in DNA sequencing). But the first thing most native English speakers will think of when they hear the word "terminator" is the time-traveling cyborg assassin played by Arnold Schwarzenegger in the 1984 film *The Terminator*. There is even a plot point in the sequel *Terminator 2: Judgment Day* where the terminator attempts to appear more human by learning alternatives to the word "affirmative" such as some of those listed here.

[100] Genericization is a similar linguistic phenomenon that occurs when a specific brand name or trademarked term becomes so widely used that it loses its exclusive association with the original product or company. Common examples in America include "Aspirin" as a catchall for pain medication and "Kleenex" as a catchall for tissues.

recently watched a Superman film for the first time in her life. Immediately after, she noticed pop culture references to the character she had previously ignored. It became clear to her that "kryptonite," the name of the fictional substance that acts as Superman's only major weakness[101] in most versions of his story, could be used as a byword for any major exploitable weakness. The much-older term "Achilles' heel" serves a similar purpose, and our students were already familiar with it because they had learned about Homer and *The Iliad* in school.[102] Though all of them had heard of the character Superman, none knew the lore surrounding him well enough to recognize what "kryptonite" meant in this context. What surprised me most was that though the lesson planner had only recently learned this word herself, she already took its reappropriated use for granted and expected our students to recognize it too.

Pragmatics and Implied Communication

If you could get a classroom full of foreign English learners to memorize an English dictionary, practice all grammar perfectly, and speak with flawless native-like pronunciation, they still would not communicate as native speakers do. They would be missing the cultural parts of English communication, the parts we pick up on and start replicating through exposure to pragmatic patterns. It encompasses everything

---

[101]   Superman is an alien from the fictional planet Krypton who, under the influence of Earth's yellow sun, gains superpowers that make him functionally invulnerable. Kryptonite is a green radioactive mineral substance from Krypton that interacts with his alien biology to nullify his superpowers, causing him immense pain or even death with exposure.

[102]   When Achilles was a baby, his mother held him by his heel and dipped him in the River Styx. This made his entire body invulnerable except for the part of his heel she held him by. This proved to be his downfall when he was lethally shot in the back of the heel by a poisoned arrow.

communicated without being explicitly stated. Meaning is not limited to just what can be inferred by words and their arrangements. It relies on familiarity with countless externalities the communicator assumes will be shared by whom they speak or write to. These implicit assumptions fill in missing information, such as context and shared background knowledge, to convey information indirectly, reducing the cognitive effort required for comprehension.[103]

If a stranger enters your house without knocking or ringing the doorbell, the first thing you blurt out in surprise might be, "Who the hell are you, and why are you in my house?!" These are extremely straightforward questions with clear, explicit meaning (with some urgency and emphasis added by the inclusion of the swear phrase "the hell"): "Identify yourself and state your reason for being here." However, there's also an unstated pragmatic meaning to these words. We cannot infer the full intended meaning from the words alone. We must also know the tone, culture, and specific setting in which the words are being spoken.

In the context of unexpected intrusion into a private space, the meaning behind "Who are you? Why are you in my house?" is something more like: "You are a stranger to me, and that means you should not be in my house because it is a private space where only people I know and am prepared to see are welcome. The fact that you do not fall into that category causes me to assume that you are a threat of some kind and intend to do me harm. I am extremely alarmed and uncomfortable with you being here. You should leave my house immediately before I take drastic action to defend my-

---

[103] Keysar, B., Barr, D. J., Balin, J. A., & Paek, T. S. (1998). Definite reference and mutual knowledge: Process models of common ground in comprehension. Journal of Memory and Language, 39(1), 1-20.

self, such as attacking you or calling the police." That's a bit more of a mouthful to blurt out in surprise. Implied meaning allows us to include more information than just that found in what we directly write or say. It saves time and effort for both speaker and listener, so long as they share enough of the same premises about how people communicate.

Think of how different the pragmatic communication would be in the above situation for someone from a culture where it is not considered rude to enter a home without permission (which is a real situation I've run into in some rural locations around the world). There might be no reason for the intruder to assume someone would be upset by this behavior. The same words would lack the context required to get the intended meaning of intrusion, alarm, and threat across. The homeowner would grow increasingly frustrated that their rude visitor would continue to ignore their verbal protests that, in their mind, they would be clearly communicating.[104]

Effective EFL teachers must instill the same social expectations that guide communication in native English-speaking countries, i.e., everything assumed to be known by all parties without being explicitly stated. It happens a thousand times in any given conversation, instantly and invisibly. The speaker works through a rapid process of determining what explicit information they have to add to what they infer the listener knows to get them to understand something new or take some new action. Teachers must even train English

---

[104] A problem faced by some people on the autism spectrum is not understanding culturally implied and pragmatic communication, such as nonverbal cues, sarcasm, irony, metaphors, and social context. They focus instead on what is explicitly stated, frequently to the point of misunderstanding. The foreign English learner is in a similar disadvantaged position if they lack cultural familiarity with the common sayings, idioms, and expectations of the people they communicate with.

learners to use body language to subtly emphasize or negate certain aspects of their communication.[105]

There is always some overlap in pragmatics between related cultures. But the gap grows as we span further distances across the globe to more culturally and linguistically alien places. Imagine how confusing the pragmatics of these common English phrases might be for learners who come from radically different cultures.

"I'd like to see you try."

The explicit meaning is that you want to witness someone attempt something. On the surface, it seems like a positive and encouraging statement. However, the implied meaning is mockery, as though the idea of being successful were so preposterous that the attempt would be entertaining to witness.

"Tell me about it."

The explicit meaning is that you want someone to elaborate on something and explain what they know. The implied meaning is that you already know about what the other person is saying or experiencing, to the point that you don't need them to tell you anything more about it. It can be used either sincerely or sarcastically.

Or consider this classic joke from the 1980 movie *Airplane!*:

---

[105] A common issue I've encountered when teaching online EFL lessons is timid students not wanting to turn on their cameras to let the rest of the group see their faces. I have to explain that learning the English language is about learning to communicate in a new holistic way. An integral part of that is unspoken visual indicators. It's not enough just to be able to hear each other's words. The quality of instruction improves when everyone can see each other's non-verbal cues to indicate emotional state and pragmatic meaning.

Randy: "Excuse me, sir. There's been a little problem in the cockpit."

Striker: "The cockpit! What is it?"

Randy: "It's the little room in the front of the plane where the pilots sit. But that's not important right now."

The joke here is that Randy thinks Striker is asking what the cockpit is instead of what *the problem* in the cockpit is. A native English speaker should immediately understand what the intended communication is and, therefore, why the misunderstanding is funny. In this situation, why would someone be asking what the cockpit is instead of what the problem is? Randy's tone indicates that the problem requires immediate attention. Problems with airplanes in mid-flight are taken seriously because they endanger the lives of everyone on board. And who the heck doesn't know what a cockpit is? Striker uses "The cockpit!" as an exclamation to indicate surprise about what's happening in the cockpit, not to change the subject of his next sentence. But a foreign English learner paying attention to only what's explicitly stated might not pick up on this. Randy's interpretation makes grammatical sense to them. Striker asked a question with the pronoun "it" immediately after mentioning the cockpit. It's logical to assume that the pronoun "it" in the question "What is it?" is replacing "the cockpit." Too many assumed externalities exist for them to receive the joke as intended.

And finally, a meta-joke about the pragmatics of pragmatics themselves:

Interviewer: "What's your greatest weakness?"

Candidate: "Interpreting the semantics of a question but ignoring the pragmatics."

Interviewer: "Could you give me an example?"

Candidate: "Yes, I could."[106]

---

[106] The interviewer isn't just asking if the candidate is *capable* of giving an example of ignoring pragmatics. They are expecting them *to* give an example. The candidate gives one by responding to the explicit meaning of the question but ignoring the implied meaning. Their response that they are capable of giving an example is, itself, the example.

CHAPTER 9

BEYOND CONVERSATIONAL FLUENCY

AT THE HIGHEST levels of English proficiency, even small deficiencies can have a large impact on communication. Though they may be understood quite well, a conversationally fluent foreign English speaker will be perceived differently than a truly fluent one by native speakers. Just being "pretty good" might not be enough for what the English learner wishes to accomplish with the language and the impression they wish to make on others.[107] Closing this gap is the hardest feat for many learners.

A conversationally fluent English speaker can get the most important aspects of what they wish to communicate across to native speakers without major impediments. They consistently say the words that mean roughly what they intend in the right order. But this is not enough to use English exactly as a native speaker does. Their English mind operates

---

[107] The Turing Test, conceived by computer scientist Alan Turing in 1950, was meant to determine a machine's ability to exhibit human-like intelligence. Essentially, if humans cannot consistently differentiate between machine and human responses, the machine is considered to have passed the test and demonstrated artificial intelligence. Perhaps we can apply a similar standard to evaluating native-like English fluency: If native speakers cannot consistently identify anything about a speaker's use of English that makes them think they are non-native, we can consider them truly fluent.

like a webpage loading on a slow internet connection. There's considerable buffering with almost every download (listening/reading) or upload (speaking/writing). They are loading in batches of only a few words at a time, often not even in complete clauses (let alone complete sentences). Going beyond conversational fluency requires cognizing the spontaneous order of the language in larger packages of meaning that adapt in real-time expression.

A conversationally fluent English speaker can form grammatically valid sentences. However, they will often still need to check with native speakers to see if what they've constructed sounds like something a native speaker would say and gets the details of their meaning across as they intend. Being truly fluent means they do not need to worry about how a native speaker will perceive them. They trust their own analysis. They know what they intend to communicate and why the words they've chosen for the task constitute the best option. To speak or write English like a native speaker means to give close to zero indication that you've learned English as a foreign language and portray comfort and intentionality in all aspects of communication.

It is even possible for foreign English learners to surpass the standards of native speakers. Native speakers repeat many simple mistakes in common speech, hardly ever realizing it. They might take for granted that they are always understood and put little effort into optimizing their communication. Their phrasing often becomes cliché or redundant. They default to the same words repeatedly and have little reason to improve.

True fluency goes beyond the common EFL imperative of speaking in a widely accepted manner for the highest chance of being broadly understood. Advanced communication is about being understood by specific people in specific ways. It eventually results in a unique voice or style for the speaker, which is something that even many native English speakers never fully develop. How they *speak* English becomes a tangible representation of how they *think* in English, which requires total fluency.

Subtle Lexical Variation

Since English is loaded with near-synonyms that cannot be used interchangeably, fluent speakers must discern when and where to use one word or another. Overusing a small lexicon is one of the telltale signs of a non-native speaker who is still not totally comfortable with English. It can get the job done, but it detracts from nuance, clarity, personality, and the ability to recognize the uniqueness of the mind behind the words. For example, if you are describing the way someone spoke to you, it would be considered stylistically poor in most cases to repeat the word "said" many times, even if it's an accurate description.

A conversationally fluent English speaker might phrase such a paragraph like this:

> "She **said** I needed to meet her at the airport, which she **said** would be busy that time of day. She **said** the flight would be landing at around 6:30 p.m. However, she also **said** that it would take some time for her to get off the plane and collect her luggage. She **said** not to get there too early, or I'd be waiting around for a while. When I asked her how long she expected it to take, she **said** at least 20 minutes."

There's nothing technically wrong with this sequence of sentences. Each one is competent and practical English on its own. I would be proud of an English learner the first time they became conversationally fluent enough to spontaneously say something like this and be understood. But a native English speaker usually wouldn't convey this information like this. There would be natural variation in their choice of words, even if they didn't have any conscious intention of avoiding repetition:

> "She **said** I needed to meet her at the airport, which she **explained** would be busy that time of day. She **told me** the flight would be landing at around 6:30 p.m. However, she also **let me know** that it would take some time for her to get off the plane and collect her luggage. She **warned me** not to get there too early, or I'd be waiting around for a while. When I asked her how long she expected it to take, she **answered** at least 20 minutes."

The basic sentence structure is the same, but there is a notable stylistic improvement. Now, we have only one instance of "said." All others have been replaced by words or phrases that are more specific and stylized: "Explained,"[108] "told me,"[109] "let me know,"[110] "warned me,"[111] and "answered."[112]

---

[108] To explain is to elaborate in greater detail the nature of something or how it works.

[109] Telling is a more direct and active way of saying something to someone, which is why it usually needs the object receiving the telling to be explicitly stated.

[110] The phrasal verb "to let know" means to casually reveal information to someone.

[111] To warn is to advise someone about danger.

[112] To answer is to satisfy a request for information.

Each gives a bit more detail to the type of "saying" that is happening. The extra detail in these nuanced verb choices is not totally necessary for the functional meaning to get across. The native speaker defaults to adding variety because repeating "said" so many times would sound jarring and uncomfortable. The foreign learner must adopt a similar unconscious stylistic response to English vocabulary, which will be the product of being exposed to a varied lexicography enough and having made a conscious effort to use other options when an easier term would have sufficed. Eventually, using them ceases to require conscious effort.

A good exercise for the conversationally fluent English speaker seeking true fluency is to see how many detailed ways they can comfortably communicate the same idea.

Simple: "I am angry at my boss for not giving me a raise."

Detailed: "I feel awful right now. My manager wouldn't agree to start paying me more, in spite of everything I do here."

Simple: "He was unhappy about the situation."

Detailed: "He got disappointed with how things turned out. In his heart, he knew there should have been a more equitable outcome for everyone involved."

Simple: "I wouldn't have enough bravery for a divorce without that affair."

Detailed: "If he hadn't had that affair, I would never have grown brave enough to accept that our marriage was over and pursue divorce.

There is, however, a counterpoint to infusing variety into speech and writing. Sometimes, we need to use the same word or phrasing several times in quick succession. Sometimes, the precise intended meaning depends on doing so. If you're leading a symposium on the nature and causes of anger, changing the terminology you use in every sentence might not be stylistically appropriate. Your audience might get confused and think you are talking about more than one concept when you intentionally refer back to the same emotional state each time. Here's an example of what not to do:

> "**Anger** is an emotional response to a perceived threat or injustice. When a person experiences **indignation**, the body releases adrenaline and other stress hormones. These biological changes caused by **rage** help prepare the body for immediate action. **Hostility** is also associated with increased focus and narrowed attention. However, keep in mind that the way people express **fury** can vary from person to person."

Can you spot the problem? Anger,[113] indignation,[114] rage,[115] hostility,[116] and fury[117] are five related concepts. In many communication contexts, swapping some of these terms around in the right places would be appropriate to cre-

[113] Anger is the base category for the emotion of displeasure in response to perceived external threats, frustration, or provocation.

[114] Indignation is an angered response to injustice, unfair treatment, or a violation of principles or values with a sense of moral outrage. It is a more specific and purpose-driven type of anger that stems from a perceived attack on dignity.

[115] "Rage" indicates the most intense, ongoing, uncontrollable, and violent extreme end of anger, usually implying a loss of control beyond any beneficial utility that controlled anger might have brought.

[116] "Hostility" refers to a deep-rooted sense of antagonism, animosity, or opposition, e.g., the desire to do harm (physical or emotional). However, hostility can also be a passive quality. You don't need to be under the throes of anger to desire to do harm someone or something.

[117] Fury is an outburst of wild irrational anger, like rage without the commitment. It can be likened to temporary madness or insanity.

ate more nuance and avoid dull repetition. But in this case, it contributes to confusion. Are we talking about the same thing in these five cases? Are we trying to indicate that fury has qualities that indignation does not? Or are we just arbitrarily swapping terms around and muddling the message?

A native English speaker would recognize that this is a context where repeatedly referring to the same term is necessary for clarity. They would minimize the dullness by inserting pronouns where appropriate and even restructuring sentences to avoid referring to the subject repeatedly.

> "**Anger** is an emotional response to a perceived threat or injustice. When a person experiences **it**, the body releases adrenaline and other stress hormones. These biological changes caused by **this emotion** help prepare the body for immediate action. **Anger** is also associated with increased focus and narrowed attention. However, keep in mind that the way people express **their anger** can vary from person to person."

Instead of a slew of unnecessarily nuanced near-synonyms, we have an intentionally narrow focus on anger and other placeholders that refer back to it: "anger," "it," "this emotion," "anger," and "their anger." Is it a bit duller than the previous nuanced version? Sure. But its meaning is now clear and controlled.

Phrasal Verbs and Idioms

Many common English expressions don't make much sense when you break them down into constituent parts, but native English speakers still know how to use them. They are idiomatic combinations of often unrelated verbs, adverbs, and prepositions that take on emergent meaning not present in any part individually. Instead of trying to learn every possible phrasal verb by rote, English learners should try to see the internal logic of the particular combination of words and how it is used. Effective English teachers should encourage their students to find the likely reasoning behind each phrasal arrangement and adopt the same mental imagery as native speakers to internally represent them. Even a made-up justification for a phrase can still serve as a good mnemonic device.

Anyone can see what is meant by "checking **into**" or "checking **out of** a hotel." "In" and "out" and their derivatives signify obvious physical relationships between you and the hotel. "Looking **forward** to" something conjures an image of peering hopefully into the future in anticipation of a positive occurrence. The use of the word "forward" is not arbitrary; it just requires some figurative interpretation to avoid interpreting it as the literal act of someone staring straight ahead.

What about something less clear, though, such as "messing something **up**"? The image I conjure when I hear this phrase is that of someone taking something orderly and throwing it up into the air in chaotic, disconnected pieces. "Messing something **down**" sounds odd to a native English speaker. However, "talking **down**" or giving a "dressing **down**" to someone is much clearer when you understand that these phrases mean lowering someone's mood or social status. The adverbial directions "up" and "down" contribute to the meaning of these phrases. Likewise, "settling **down**" makes intuitive sense. I picture something going from an active state to a less active one. "Down" is the direction things naturally get pulled in when they stop resisting. Why do we say "give **up**" to indicate surrender? A tenuous connection could be putting one's hands in the air to indicate compliance and non-hostility or even throwing one's hands up in frustration. When we "get **over** something," it's as though there is an obstacle blocking us from moving forward. If we can manage to laboriously climb over it, it won't be an obstacle any longer.

The same applies to all idiomatic expressions, no matter how non-sensical they might seem out of context from their origins.

Idiom: "**Hit** the hay" or "**hit** the sack."

I think of an exhausted farmer falling asleep in a haystack after working all day in his barn or a tired person falling in a stupor onto an overstuffed mattress (i.e., "sack").

Idiom: "**Hit** the books."

I think of a student aggressively cramming all night to study for a test the next morning.

Idiom: "**Hit** the bricks."

I think of someone's feet slamming against the pavement as they rush out of a building onto the street outside.

None of these images need to have anything to do with the actual origin of these idioms. They still feel appropriate, and they ensure that I use them correctly. The word "hit" in each example doesn't need to have anything to do with literally hitting something (though it can). It just needs to denote an emotion associated with hitting.

Idiom: "Going to the dogs."

What do we usually give to dogs? The scraps of food at the dinner table that we don't want and think are unfit for human consumption. The bone after the steak is gone and other unsightly leftovers are what go to the dogs. Anything that is "going to the dogs" is what's left after all the good parts are gone.

Spontaneously Shifting Parts of Speech

As noted, one major advantage of English is its clear and consistent syntax. This is largely due to how flexible its parts of speech are, which is a consequence of its limited range of morphological changes. English often changes nothing or little about a word when transitioning between noun, adjective, verb, or adverb, so the context of where the word goes in a sentence is what primarily reveals its role. Adding or removing a word before or after another can completely change the structure and meaning of the sentence.

"I am going to the **city**."

What part of speech does the word "city" take in this sentence? It's clearly a noun. It's the place where you are going. It's the object of "to go." The only places you can go to are nouns.

Here's the same sentence with one word added to the end:

"I am going to the city **center**."

What changes about the sentence's structure because we now have "center" after "city"? What part of speech is "city" now? Nothing has changed about the word "city" itself. We didn't, for instance, add a suffix that might indicate something new about its relationship to the rest of the sentence. Yet, it's clear to native English speakers that it's no longer a noun. "City" must be an adjective here because it's modifying the new noun "center" we placed after it. Every native English speaker knows that having two nouns in sequence wouldn't make any sense and that adjectives always precede their nouns. Together, the words "city center" form a noun phrase. They are still indicating the place where you are going.

What if we added the common adjectival suffix –*ish* or –*esque*? Does "I am going to the city**ish** center" mean something different? Yes. It means you are going to a center with qualities resembling those of a city. That's not the same as going to the city's center.

This can get even more confusing for the foreign learner when we include prepositions that only work for certain parts of speech in a sentence with words filling ambiguous roles:

Correct: "I am going **to** a meeting."

Also correct: "I am going **to** the office."

These two sentences have parallel structure. The only difference is the noun we indicate we are going to: either to a meeting or to the office. Both function as locations in this type of construction. But what happens if we change the preposition to "for"?

Correct: "I am going **for** a meeting."

Incorrect: "I am going **for** the office."

Now, something stands out as being different between these two. The preposition "for" is used in this context to indicate the purpose of something. In the previous example, the preposition "to" indicated location. The nouns "meeting" and "office" function as locations in the mind of an English speaker. However, "office" is not normally used as a noun denoting purpose.[118] "Meeting" is. You can go somewhere to have a meeting; you cannot go somewhere to have an office.

---

[118] Under the right communication conditions, a fluent English speaker can make "the office" work as a purpose for something, thereby enabling

Articles can also affect parts of speech and when a word choice is valid.

Correct: "I am going for **meeting**."[119]

Incorrect: "I am going for **office**."

How does removing the articles from these sentences change their meaning? The role that the object noun ("meeting" or "office") plays is now different. One of them works, and one does not. "Meeting" now functions as a gerund, a noun derived from the continuous conjugation of the verb "to meet." Yet, it is still written and pronounced the same as in the previous examples. "Office" cannot be used this way because it is not derived from a verb.

English speakers can quickly change what they intend to say, even as they are in the middle of saying it, due to the language's flexible phrasing. In text, an editor can often add, remove, or change just a few words in a sentence and restructure it to mean something different.

"**I will pay** the fee at the entrance of the amusement park."

This is a straightforward indicative statement conjugated in the future simple tense. But look how the structure and meaning change if we remove the first two words:

"**Pay** the fee at the entrance of the amusement park."

The mood of the sentence has changed to imperative. It's a command for you (the implied subject) to pay. The verb

---

the preposition "for" to work with it. For example: "I am going to the computer store to look at buying some things for **the office**" could be shortened to "I am going for **the office**."

[119] Although this is a grammatically valid construction, a more natural way for native English speakers to say this might be, "I am going to meet someone." This sounds better because it has an object with "meet." "For networking" would be a choice that works better without an object.

"pay" has not changed at all, and neither has anything else about the rest of the sentence. The big change in meaning is communicated merely by a lack of other words preceding "pay."

Compare these alternatives showing a similar change in structure by the inclusion of an additional word:

"**I finished** working today."

"I **am** finished working today."

In the first example, "finished" is a verb conjugated in the past simple tense. In the second, "finished" is a participle: an adjective derived from the verb "to finish." It indicates that the qualities of the verb have been applied to the subject "I." The only thing indicating the difference in structure is the inclusion of the verb "am." The native English brain automatically recategorizes the role of "finished" as a verb or adjective based on whether it sees a verb preceding it. It knows two conjugated verbs in sequence would not work, so the second ambiguous verb "finished" must be functioning as an adjective instead.

What mistake is an English learner making if they ask you, "What **misses** from your professor's house?" The correct phrasing would be "What **is missing** from your professor's house?" The speaker has tried to use the present simple conjugation of the verb "to miss" as "misses." They probably interpreted "is missing" as the present continuous conjugation and incorrectly assumed either option would be valid. In this context, "missing" is an adjective derived from the verb. It is no different than asking, "Have you found the **missing** book?" The confusion arises from the fact that the continuous verb, the adjective, and even the gerund[120] are spelled and pronounced the same.

Because "missing" is treated as an adjective, this sentence works like "What **is great** about your professor's house?" But since "great" is not derived from a verb, it's more obvious that we could never phrase it as "What **greats** about your professor's house?" "To great" is not a verb.

Complex and Compound Sentences

The rearrangeable nature of English sentences is a major part of the language's adaptability as a form of global communication. Its flexible structure allows for simplification and adaptation among non-native speakers with diverse preferences for expressing themselves.[121] Speakers can reorder and modify sentence components to convey meaning precisely as they intend, even in the middle of speaking or writing. Global English learners must eventually cease trying to perfectly plan out every word they are going to say before opening their mouths or putting their pens to paper. They must trust that when they begin the sentence, they will find their way to a grammatically valid and stylistically appropriate ending as they go.

Complex sentences are formed when speakers add more information than could be conveyed by simple ones. But this must be done in a tactful way. The more moving parts you have in a sentence, the more important style becomes for conveying all its information effectively. English learners might

---

[120] E.g., "The search team has been looking all week, but they still haven't found all the **missing** and unaccounted for."

[121] Seidlhofer, B. (2005). English as a lingua franca. ELT Journal, 59(4), 339-341.

easily grasp the most basic sentence structures in English but feel lost when trying to stuff in more detail beyond what the simple subject-verb-object (SVO) format allows for. The next level of complexity is to link two SVO sentences together via a comma and coordinating conjugation:

"I like traveling."

"I like reading."[122]

These two simple sentences can easily be combined into the compound sentence, "I like traveling, **and** I like reading." We can also put more information in simple sentences by adding phrases to the end in the form of direct and indirect objects for verbs.

"I like traveling **to the beach**."

"I like traveling **to the mountains**."

These two can similarly be combined: "I like traveling to the beach, **and** I like traveling to the mountains." Instead of presenting two different ideas about liking traveling to the beach and liking traveling to the mountains, the two belong to part of the same idea because they are in the same sentence. The meaning has subtly changed, even though the speaker is saying almost exactly the same words.

In most cases, it would be unnecessary to restate the shared gerund "traveling" since it applies equally to both objects ("to the beach" and "to the mountain"). You are saying more words than necessary and conveying the same amount of information. A native speaker would likely only do so for

---

[122] There is some common confusion when using participles as the objects of verbs. In these cases, the gerunds "traveling" and "reading" are not continuous conjugations of verbs. They are nouns designating those activities. Similarly, if we conjugate these same sentences with the infinitive form of these verbs (i.e., "I like to travel" and "I like to read"), "to travel" and "to read" still function as nouns. The only functioning verb in these sentences is "like."

intentional emphasis through repetition. Most of the time, they would default to "I like traveling **to the beach and the mountains.**"

What is the practical limit on additional phrases that can be tacked onto complex and compound sentences? There is no rule saying that you have to stop at a certain point before the sentence becomes ungrammatical. It's a matter of whether stuffing more details into the same sentence contributes to the quality of the communication or detracts from it. Any sentence that goes on so long that it's hard to conceptualize it as a single idea is a run-on sentence. You may even forget how it began by the time you reach the end:

> "I like traveling to the beach with my friends so that we can go swimming in the salty water while the sun is bright after we have a big picnic in the sand with lots of sandwiches and soda that…"

There's no reason to force all this information into the same sentence and imply that it must all be part of the same idea. It leaves the audience desperate for a break and wondering why the speaker is still droning on about details of increasingly lesser importance. A run-on sentence has no sense of prioritization once the subject and predicate have been established. Everything else just gets tacked onto the action being taken. What is the idea the audience is supposed to come away with? That you like traveling to the beach with your friends? Or something about salty water, bright sun, and picnics of sandwiches and soda? Any of these could be important, depending on what the writer/speaker has decided to communicate. If they were broken up into different sentences, an information hierarchy would be easier to establish:

"**I like** traveling to the beach with my friends. **We go** there to swim in the salty water under the bright sun. Afterward, **we have** a big picnic in the sand with lots of sandwiches and soda."

The structure of each of these three sentences is simple and straightforward. All we have done is partitioned the excessive amount of information from one run-on sentence into three sentences of manageable size and order.

The problem of run-on sentences gets even more pronounced with periodic sentences that stuff all the extraneous detail into the middle and don't allow for grammatical completeness until we reach the end. The listener must stay in suspense from the setup of the subject and pay close attention to when the ending finally comes, revealing the action the subject is taking.

"**My friends,** who enjoy swimming in the salty water while the sun is bright after we have a big picnic in the sand with lots of sandwiches and soda, **are my favorite people to travel to the beach with.**"

Emphasis, Intonation, and Tone

Native English speakers will sometimes add semantically unnecessary words for emphasis. Foreign learners might, at first, overlook the importance of these seemingly superfluous additions. Or worse, in attempting to sound more native, they might fall into the habit of using them in inappropriate ways that only emphasize how foreign English still is for them.

What is the semantic difference between these sentences?

"**What's** your favorite book?"

"**What is** your favorite book?"

They mean the same thing. The first option just slightly abbreviates the sentence by making a contraction of "what" and "is" with "what's." You could say the contracted version might be considered slightly less formal. But there are times when a native English speaker would choose the non-contracted version for stylistic emphasis.

"Hey man. **What's** your favorite book? Is it *The Catcher in the Rye?*"

"No, that's not my favorite book."

"Well, then, **what** *is* your favorite book?"

There's a subtle but important difference in the second iteration of the question because it is in response to a negation. Emphasizing the "is" contrasts it more against what was just stated. The intentional lack of contraction emphasizes the word "is" in juxtaposition to what "is not" the favorite book. The contracted version of the question would lose that nuance. Even emphasizing the contracted "what's" would not capture the same effect.

A similar effect happens with verbs when we intentionally include "do" as an auxiliary verb where it is not strictly required.[123] "Do" is only required when asking present simple questions or answering such questions in the negative form. We usually omit it when answering in the affirmative form with simple declarative sentences unless we want to emphasize the answer to contrast with the negative option:

"I knew it! You never cared about me at all!"

"You're wrong. I **do** care about you."

---

[123] Known by linguists as do-support, do-insertion, or periphrastic do.

It can even add strength to an affirmative statement without anything to contrast it against:

"You're so good at playing that song."

"Well, I should hope so. I **do** practice two hours a day, after all."

Even without adding words, intonated emphasis can alter meaning. "This is **the** book to read" (without stress on any individual word) indicates which book someone is meant to read. "This is *the* book to read" (with stress on "the") makes its definite article hyperbolic, indicating a book that stands out above all others, as though it is incomparably superior.

English speakers can also move the clauses in a sentence around to subtly influence the meaning and tone. This emphasis affects what words they interpret as most important or in contrast to something else. Consider the following construction options for the same short sentence:

1. "However, it seems that you didn't get the job."

2. "It seems, however, that you didn't get the job."

3. "However, you didn't get the job, it seems."

4. "It seems that you didn't get the job, however."

Can you tell what the subtle difference is for each? Read them aloud. How does your intonation change as you say each one? Where do you naturally stress words or pause? These are elements of native English communication that likely won't come easily to even a conversationally fluent foreign learner.

We have three basic phrases or pieces of information to arrange:

• "however"

• "it seems"

• "you didn't get the job"

Which of these three will you make most important? What are you contrasting each against? How do they affect the meaning of one another through the relationships they form?

"**However**, it seems that you didn't get the job."

In this first example, the natural emphasis falls on the first word "however." It draws our attention to the fact that this statement will contrast something previously stated. Spoken aloud, a native English speaker might say that first word a bit slower and louder than the rest of the sentence. They will pause where the comma falls after "however" to create a small sense of separation, strengthening its importance.

"**It seems**, however, **that you didn't get the job**."

The second example is constructed to leave the audience in suspense partway through. We now have two commas that act as parentheses to suspend the "however" in the middle of the sentence. By placing this interrupting "however" between two other two pieces of information, we have to wait until the end of the sentence to figure out what the conclusion of the setup "it seems" will be. It seems something. What does it seem? I can't wait to find out. Oooh, but first, I have to wait for the "however," which reminds me that whatever follows will contrast what I already thought to be true. I didn't get the job?!

"**However, you didn't get the job**, it seems."

In this construction, the fact that "it seems" you didn't get the job is treated like an afterthought. It's the least important part of the sentence because it comes last after a complete thought has already been expressed. "However, you didn't get the job" can already stand on its own. The audience is inclined to believe the communication is finished at that point unless the speaker decides to keep going and add some extraneous detail, such as that everything already stated is only what *seems* to be the case.

"**It seems that you didn't get the job**, however."

This is a reflection of the first example. It's also the closest to a simple sentence structure. The only difference is that "however" comes at the end, indicating that it's undeserving of emphasis. If it came at the beginning like before, it would indicate a pattern interrupt to catch the audience's attention and inform them that something contradictory was coming. This time, we say the complete sentence first; then, we gently remind the audience that the thing we just said also happens to contrast something else. A native speaker wouldn't say this "however" aloud with nearly as much pause or emphasis as they would with a "however" at the start of the sentence.

TAKEAWAY

PUTTING IT ALL INTO PRACTICE

THROUGHOUT MY WANDERING EFL career, I've made it my mission to call attention to the inadequacies discussed in this book. Unfortunately, I have found that most people involved in their countries' respective education programs are not receptive to improvement, nor are the Western academics who control the production and dissemination of sanctioned information regarding the global state of EFL. Few people in positions of educational authority like being told that the way they've been doing things could be improved. The older they get, the more enmeshed they become in broken systems. They are more interested in maintaining the status quo and protecting their positions than in helping people learn to communicate in English and gain all the social and economic benefits that would come from it. Superior ideas will not matter so long as administration is immune to amending.

That's why I have primarily written for the individual who cares about their educational impact and is willing to consider that there may be better ways to practice their craft. I don't expect systemic institutional change, but *you* have the power to make a difference in the lives of the English seekers in the country or countries you operate in. Even if you are beholden to rules and a standardized curriculum, you can still make learning English engaging and enjoyable (and, therefore, more effective at imparting practical fluency). You can evolve your approach beyond local standards.

A healthy alternative to the conventional EFL approach is guided group conversations that focus on the types of English discussions learners would otherwise not have the opportunity to participate in. With your guidance, such conversations take English out of the realm of ordinary interaction and into more creative subjects that stimulate original thought. Learners get to discuss ideas they otherwise never would, which directly contributes to the mind-expanding and limitation-shattering effects of learning a global language.

These group classes often begin with a fairly typical approach to English conversation, but they don't stay there long. Examples might include:

Travel Philosophy and Lifestyle

- Discussing the learners' own travel experiences, ambitions, lessons, destinations, and cultural encounters
- Role-playing travel scenarios and practicing language skills in real-life travel situations
- Identifying different types of travelers and how they differ, such as vacationers, tourists, business travelers, expatriates, and perpetual travelers.

Critical Thinking Skills

- Identifying cognitive biases and logical fallacies that prevent people from seeing the world clearly

- Engaging in debates and exploring different perspectives on contested issues
- Examining why we think the way we do about the things we care about

Once the group has gotten somewhat comfortable with the topic's vocabulary and basic themes, we open the discussion to matters deeper and more meaningful. The goal is to have the learners organically continue the discussion in English without constant prompting and an artificially limited range of expression. As teachers, we provide the conversation framework and monitor how well the learners use the English they know in this context. We guide the conversation in ways that require the learners to think in ways they never have before.

Their initial inclination is to say what they think they are supposed to say in every conversation. They limit their English to standard expressions they are 100% sure they are saying correctly and that are appropriate for the prompt. Though this may look like good English externally, it doesn't do much to challenge and grow their English abilities. What they need more than anything is the opportunity to generate stimulating original thoughts in English, the kinds of sentences that no teacher could have prepped them to say.

Thoughtful prompts include detailed, open-ended questions like:

> "Why do you think so many people talk about wanting to travel someday, but relatively few people ever actually do it? Is it just practical issues like the price of airfare or the difficulty of getting a visa? Maybe there are some psychological elements to it too. A lot of people are uncomfortable with suddenly changing every-

thing about their lives. Many people are afraid of what might happen to them in an unknown environment on the other side of the planet."

"How many different ways do you think people let pressures and biases from their culture affect their thinking? Are you more or less likely to like the same food, clothes, and music as the people you grow up around? Do you think people are automatically prejudiced against people and ideas from foreign cultures, especially if it's a country with a history of conflict with their own? How do you form sound conclusions without unfair biases about these things?"

You can imagine how many emergent opportunities for expression this kind of Socratic questioning[124] can lead to. But it only works so long as a few basic conditions are met:

1. The majority of the students participating must be comfortable speaking up. If everyone is too shy to speak, the conversation tends to be dominated by the teacher(s) and one or two outgoing learners. The teachers must do what they can to facilitate participation from reluctant students, which is a task usually

---

[124] The Socratic method of teaching is one in which the teacher generally assumes ignorance and guides students in arriving at knowledge by asking probing questions that require them to elucidate the subject, defining terms as they intend them, filling in any gaps in their understanding, and correcting any contradictions they didn't realize they were making. One of the most basic ways to apply this with EFL learners is to ask them to come up with their own descriptions (not dictionary definitions or direct native language translations) for the way they use nuanced English terms before constructing sentences and using them in advanced discourse. You'll find that even many native English speakers struggle with this, so doing it regularly can help foreign learners excel beyond their abilities.

better suited for the non-native teacher since they will be seen as more familiar and less intimidating to the learners.

2. The topics covered in each class must be things the learners are genuinely interested in discussing. They need to find them intrinsically rewarding to talk about, which means they can't just be participating as an arbitrary exercise in using English. They won't have the right emotional motivation and will be waiting to be told what to say or do. They will revert to the mindset of parroting the correct answer for praise or a good grade.

A recent group discussion on the differences between masculinity and femininity went into some considerably deep territory with the ten or so students being led by me and my non-native teaching partner. The conversation started with describing traits generally associated more with men or women respectively. The learners quickly adopted terms like "assertiveness," "vulnerability," "aggressive," "nurturing," "agreeable," "testosterone, "estrogen," "attraction," "women's rights," "feminism," "stereotype," and "sexual dimorphism."

At a glance, these don't seem like high-priority words for English learners to acquire and use in everyday life. It's not like they are going to need to say "sexual dimorphism" on a daily basis. But these learners were well past the point of adding new words to their vocabulary. Their use of English was already functional or beyond. They needed to focus on learning to think as English speakers.

In how many ways can an English learner examine the term "sexual dimorphism" to arrive at its meaning? First comes the adjective "sexual." Perhaps the learners are only accustomed to hearing this term used in reference to acts related to having sex. They know about sexual intimacy or a sexual dance. But now, it is being used in a physiological context to describe the anatomy of the human sexes.

Next is a word they probably have not heard before: "dimorphism." Guessing its meaning requires paying attention to context and common affixes. *Di*– is a prefix that means two, twice, or double. The learners have probably seen it in other words like "**di**chotomy," "**di**ad," "**di**vorce," or "**di**oxide." What does "morph" mean? It relates to changing form. When the Power Rangers famously shout, "It's morphin' time!" they are proclaiming their intention to change form into their superpowered suits (which could be a useful reference if the learners are familiar with this element of 90s American pop culture). English morphology, similarly, is the study of forms that words in English can take to change their meaning. The common suffix –*ism*, as they should already know, refers to a system of ideas about something. "Dimorphism," therefore, indicates a system of two forms something can take.

Knowing all this, can the learners derive the meaning of "sexual dimorphism"? Maybe not on their first guess (unless they have a background in biology), but the guessing process is nonetheless important. Frequently, learners will come up with guesses that aren't exactly correct but that are still reasonable and have a clear, logical thought process behind them. This is a good habit for them to develop and much better than refusing to try to understand a new term at all.

Once I explain to them that this term describes the two differentiated forms males and females of a species can take (and use it several times when referencing the physiological differences between human men and women), they are un-

likely to ever forget it.[125] They now have a new way of thinking about this common subject, something they probably encounter in some form every day but never deeply consider.
More importantly, they have practiced deriving the meaning
of unfamiliar terms from context and etymology. They will
be more willing to try it with unknown terms in future situations, even if their trusty teachers aren't there to guide them.
They gradually adopt the same strategies native English
speakers unconsciously use to broaden their vocabulary.

My teaching partner and I soon had the learners considering how the differences between men and women affect people, like how they might conform or be exceptions to gender
stereotypes and whether that's due to cultural influences or
natural demeanor. Then I asked the group something unexpected: "Why do you think men in some countries are four
times as likely as women to commit suicide?"[126] After a fair
amount of deliberation, they came up with some speculative
answers. Perhaps, for either physiological or social reasons,
men might be less free to express their deepest emotions.
Maybe men have a harder time finding a sense of purpose in
life. One student bluntly suggested, "Men are just better at
killing themselves than women. They are more determined
to follow through with decisions because they are more as-

---

[125] To test learners' etymological understanding of a new term, you can
change the variables and ask how it would alter the word. In this case,
once they understood the meaning of "sexual dimorphism," I asked how
they would describe an alien species that had three sexes instead of two.
They knew the correct answer was "sexually **trimorphic**." They know to
add the suffix –ly to "sexual" because it has changed grammatical function from an adjective to an adverb (as it is now describing an adjective
instead of a noun). "Dimorphism," meanwhile, has changed both its prefix and suffix because tri– means three and –ic denoted a quality applying or relating to a noun. If these learners ever become xenobiologists or
science fiction writers, they'll be ready.

[126] https://www.cdc.gov/suicide/suicide-data-statistics.html

sertive." Several minutes of enthralling debate followed entirely in English.

Regardless of the accuracy of their answers, this kind of disruptive, out-of-the-ordinary, yet entirely relevant questioning instigates new critical thinking (and thus contributes to English fluency). Considering the possible answers requires learners to generalize the qualities of masculinity and femininity already being discussed, compare them with their own experiences of men and women, and postulate plausible explanations for the gender-based discrepancy in suicide rates that no one has prompted them with. Most of them were unaware of this unsettling statistic and had never considered why it might be true. It helps to engrain the newly learned vocabulary because it requires them to understand and apply the concepts the words represent in original ways in their own minds. Their grammar and speaking abilities improve because they are made to spontaneously construct difficult sentences and keep pace with an evolving English conversation. Months later, the students reported that this was the most memorable lesson we had and that the memorability significantly contributed to the amount of English learning they retained from it.

This is a level of English application they would never experience in a conventional EFL setting or while taught from a dogmatic lesson plan. Learners are never forced to do something merely because it's what their textbook or school administrator says to. They participate because they trust where their teachers are leading them and are interested in going there. As a result, these dynamic conversations bring the learners through all the cognitive stages of learning: remembering, understanding, and applying basic terms all the way to analyzing, evaluating, and creating original communication.

This approach requires the collaboration of dynamic and adaptable teachers to guide the developing conversation who, like their students, must also meet a few basic criteria:

1. The teachers have to be prepared to keep the group on topic if learners wander off during conversation (without stifling their creative expression, as native English conversations naturally include unexpected lateral tangents all the time).[127]

2. They have to be ready to correct English mistakes as they occur in real-time (and provide native-language translation if a new English term is totally beyond understanding).

3. The teachers must keep the group engaged and actively contributing to the topic, which is unpredictable when subjects and participants change frequently.

If you are entrepreneurially minded, you may begin to see opportunities to brand yourself and your approach as explicitly different than what teachers in your market offer. You can boldly advertise that you offer a higher level of English fluency training (and even justify a higher price than the local norm). You can tailor how you teach to your own specialties, interests, and personality so that you will stand

---

[127] Effective EFL teachers will recognize the new opportunities for instruction each tangent brings instead of immediately trying to get the conversation back onto its predetermined course. A recent lesson that started off being about intergenerational differences eventually had the whole group passionately discussing the local and international history of social issues related to interracial marriage. Whether they learned all the specific terminology I had in mind for them about generational issues was irrelevant. There would be no test or grade on how well they'd memorized anything. What mattered was that they were passionately engaged in using English to talk in ways they never had before about a subject they cared about.

out even more in your market. You can back up your work with guarantees that your students will learn more and enjoy the process in ways they never have with conventional educators. There are always discerning learners who would gladly choose to work with someone who promises to make up for the shortcomings they have had to contend with. This was often my experience. My background and professional credentials hardly mattered. Results were all my students were after.

You may still be fortunate enough to find employment with an alternative type of organization that embraces a more effective English-teaching approach. Your employers may give you the freedom to adapt and experiment. Perhaps you are even in a position to start your own school or community organization that diverges from the norm. And, of course, freelance teaching and tutoring have never been easier, thanks to the internet. Whatever your teaching situation, I wish you well in adapting these principles to the extent possible with what you have to work with. Your job will be far more rewarding when you see rapid, practical progress in how your students use English. With greater English ability will come great opportunities in virtually all other areas of life, and you will feel greater reward from contributing to that outcome.

Made in the USA
Middletown, DE
14 October 2023